Mini

Cooper

Other great books from Veloce –

Speedpro Series
4-cylinder Engine – How To Blueprint & Build A Short Block For High Performance (Hammill)
Alfa Romeo DOHC High-performance Manual (Kartalamakis)
Alfa Romeo V6 Engine High-performance Manual (Kartalamakis)
BMC 998cc A-series Engine – How To Power Tune (Hammill)
1275cc A-series High-performance Manual (Hammill)
Camshafts – How To Choose & Time Them For Maximum Power (Hammill)
Competition Car Datalogging Manual, The (Templeman)
Cylinder Heads – How To Build, Modify & Power Tune Updated & Revised Edition (Burgess & Gollan)
Distributor-type Ignition Systems – How To Build & Power Tune New 3rd Edition (Hammill)
Fast Road Car – How To Plan And Build Revised & Updated Colour New Edition (Stapleton)
Ford SOHC 'Pinto' & Sierra Cosworth DOHC Engines – How To Power Tune Updated & Enlarged Edition (Hammill)
Ford V8 – How To Power Tune Small Block Engines (Hammill)
Harley-Davidson Evolution Engines – How To Build & Power Tune (Hammill)
Holley Carburetors – How To Build & Power Tune Revised & Updated Edition (Hammill)
Honda Civic Type R, High-Performance Manual (Cowland & Clifford)
Jaguar XK Engines – How To Power Tune Revised & Updated Colour Edition (Hammill)
MG Midget & Austin-Healey Sprite – How To Power Tune New 3rd Edition (Stapleton)
MGB 4-cylinder Engine – How To Power Tune (Burgess)
MGB V8 Power – How To Give Your, Third Colour Edition (Williams)
MGB, MGC & MGB V8 – How To Improve New 2nd Edition (Williams)
Mini Engines – How To Power Tune On A Small Budget Colour Edition (Hammill)
Motorcycle-engined Racing Car – How To Build (Pashley)
Motorsport – Getting Started in (Collins)
Nissan GT-R High-performance Manual, The (Gorodji)
Nitrous Oxide High-performance Manual, The (Langfield)
Rover V8 Engines – How To Power Tune (Hammill)
Sportscar & Kitcar Suspension & Brakes – How To Build & Modify Revised 3rd Edition (Hammill)
SU Carburettor High-performance Manual (Hammill)
Successful Low-Cost Rally Car, How to Build a (Young)
Suzuki 4x4 – How To Modify For Serious Off-road Action (Richardson)
Tiger Avon Sportscar – How To Build Your Own Updated & Revised 2nd Edition (Dudley)
TR2, 3 & TR4 – How To Improve (Williams)
TR5, 250 & TR6 – How To Improve (Williams)
TR7 & TR8 – How To Improve (Williams)
V8 Engine – How To Build A Short Block For High Performance (Hammill)
Volkswagen Beetle Suspension, Brakes & Chassis – How To Modify For High Performance (Hale)
Volkswagen Bus Suspension, Brakes & Chassis – How To Modify For High Performance (Hale)
Weber DCOE, & Dellorto DHLA Carburetors – How To Build & Power Tune 3rd Edition (Hammill)

Those Were The Days ... Series
Alpine Trials & Rallies 1910-1973 (Pfundner)
American Trucks of the 1950s (Mort)
Anglo-American Cars From the 1930s to the 1970s (Mort)
Austerity Motoring (Bobbitt)
Austins, The last real (Peck)
Brighton National Speed Trials (Gardiner)
British Lorries Of The 1950s (Bobbitt)
British Lorries of the 1960s (Bobbitt)
British Touring Car Championship, The (Collins)
British Police Cars (Walker)
British Woodies (Peck)
Café Racer Phenomenon, The (Walker)
Dune Buggy Phenomenon (Hale)
Dune Buggy Phenomenon Volume 2 (Hale)
Hot Rod & Stock Car Racing in Britain In The 1980s (Neil)
Last Real Austins, The, 1946-1959 (Peck)
MG's Abingdon Factory (Moylan)
Motor Racing At Brands Hatch In The Seventies (Parker)
Motor Racing At Brands Hatch In The Eighties (Parker)
Motor Racing At Crystal Palace (Collins)
Motor Racing At Goodwood In The Sixties (Gardiner)
Motor Racing At Nassau In The 1950s & 1960s (O'Neil)
Motor Racing At Oulton Park In The 1960s (McFadyen)
Motor Racing At Oulton Park In The 1970s (McFadyen)
Superprix (Page & Collins)
Three Wheelers (Bobbitt)

Enthusiast's Restoration Manual Series
Citroën 2CV, How To Restore (Porter)
Classic Car Bodywork, How To Restore (Thaddeus)
Classic British Car Electrical Systems (Astley)
Classic Car Electrics (Thaddeus)
Classic Cars, How To Paint (Thaddeus)
Reliant Regal, How To Restore (Payne)
Triumph TR2, 3, 3A, 4 & 4A, How To Restore (Williams)
Triumph TR5/250 & 6, How To Restore (Williams)
Triumph TR7/8, How To Restore (Williams)
Volkswagen Beetle, How To Restore (Tyler)
VW Bay Window Bus (Paxton)
Yamaha FS1-E, How To Restore (Watts)

Essential Buyer's Guide Series
Alfa GT (Booker)
Alfa Romeo Spider Giulia (Booker & Talbott)
BMW GS (Henshaw)
BSA Bantam (Henshaw)
BSA Twins (Henshaw)
Citroën 2CV (Paxton)
Citroën ID & DS (Heilig)
Fiat 500 & 600 (Bobbitt)
Ford Capri (Paxton)
Jaguar E-type 3.8 & 4.2-litre (Crespin)
Jaguar E-type V12 5.3-litre (Crespin)
Jaguar XJ 1995-2003 (Crespin)
Jaguar/Daimler XJ6, XJ12 & Sovereign (Crespin)
Jaguar/Daimler XJ40 (Crespin)
Jaguar XJ-S (Crespin)
MGB & MGB GT (Williams)
Mercedes-Benz 280SL-560DSL Roadsters (Bass)
Mercedes-Benz 'Pagoda' 230SL, 250SL & 280SL Roadsters & Coupés (Bass)
Mini (Paxton)
Morris Minor & 1000 (Newell)
Porsche 928 (Hemmings)
Rolls-Royce Silver Shadow & Bentley T-Series (Bobbitt)
Subaru Impreza (Hobbs)
Triumph Bonneville (Henshaw)
Triumph Stag (Mort & Fox)
Triumph TR6 (Williams)
VW Beetle (Cservenka & Copping)
VW Bus (Cservenka & Copping)
VW Golf GTI (Cservenka & Copping)

Auto-Graphics Series
Fiat-based Abarths (Sparrow)
Jaguar MKI & II Saloons (Sparrow)
Lambretta Li Series Scooters (Sparrow)

Rally Giants Series
Audi Quattro (Robson)
Austin Healey 100-6 & 3000 (Robson)
Fiat 131 Abarth (Robson)
Ford Escort MkI (Robson)
Ford Escort RS Cosworth & World Rally Car (Robson)
Ford Escort RS1800 (Robson)
Lancia Stratos (Robson)
Mini Cooper/Mini Cooper S (Robson)
Peugeot 205 T16 (Robson)
Subaru Impreza (Robson)
Toyota Celica GT4 (Robson)

WSC Giants
Ferrari 312P & 312PB (Collins & McDonough)

General
1½-litre GP Racing 1961-1965 (Whitelock)
AC Two-litre Saloons & Buckland Sportscars (Archibald)
Alfa Romeo Giulia Coupé GT & GTA (Tipler)
Alfa Romeo Montreal – The dream car that came true (Taylor)
Alfa Romeo Montreal – The Essential Companion (Taylor)
Alfa Tipo 33 (McDonough & Collins)
Alpine & Renault – The Development Of The Revolutionary Turbo F1 Car 1968 to 1979 (Smith)
Anatomy Of The Works Minis (Moylan)
André Lefebvre, and the cars he created at Voisin and Citroën (Beck)
Armstrong-Siddeley (Smith)
Autodrome (Collins & Ireland)
Automotive A-Z, Lane's Dictionary Of Automotive Terms (Lane)
Automotive Mascots (Kay & Springate)
Bahamas Speed Weeks, The (O'Neil)
Bentley Continental, Corniche And Azure (Bennett)
Bentley MkVI, Rolls-Royce Silver Wraith, Dawn & Cloud/Bentley R & S-Series (Nutland)
BMC Competitions Department Secrets (Turner, Chambers & Browning)
BMW 5-Series (Cranswick)
BMW Z-Cars (Taylor)
BMW Boxer Twins 1970-1995 Bible, The (Falloon)
Britains Farm Model Balers & Combines 1967-2007, Pocket Guide to (Pullen)
Britains Farm Model & Toy Tractors 1998-2008, Pocket Guide to (Pullen)
British 250cc Racing Motorcycles (Pereira)
British Cars, The Complete Catalogue Of, 1895-1975 (Culshaw & Horrobin)
BRM – A Mechanic's Tale (Salmon)
BRM V16 (Ludvigsen)
BSA Bantam Bible, The (Henshaw)
Bugatti Type 40 (Price)
Bugatti 46/50 Updated Edition (Price & Arbey)
Bugatti T44 & T49 (Price & Arbey)
Bugatti 57 2nd Edition (Price)
Caravans, The Illustrated History 1919-1959 (Jenkinson)
Caravans, The Illustrated History From 1960 (Jenkinson)
Carrera Panamericana, La (Tipler)
Chrysler 300 – America's Most Powerful Car 2nd Edition (Ackerson)
Chrysler PT Cruiser (Ackerson)
Citroën DS (Bobbitt)
Classic British Car Electrical Systems (Astley)
Cliff Allison – From The Fells To Ferrari (Gauld)
Cobra – The Real Thing! (Legate)
Concept Cars, How to illustrate and design (Dewey)
Cortina – Ford's Bestseller (Robson)
Coventry Climax Racing Engines (Hammill)
Daimler SP250 New Edition (Long)
Datsun Fairlady Roadster To 280ZX – The Z-Car Story (Long)
Diecast Toy Cars of the 1950s & 1960s (Ralston)
Dino – The V6 Ferrari (Long)
Dodge Challenger & Plymouth Barracuda (Grist)
Dodge Charger – Enduring Thunder (Ackerson)
Dodge Dynamite! (Grist)
Donington (Boddy)
Draw & Paint Cars – How To (Gardiner)
Drive On The Wild Side, A – 20 Extreme Driving Adventures From Around The World (Weaver)
Ducati 750 Bible, The (Falloon)
Ducati 860, 900 And Mille Bible, The (Falloon)
Dune Buggy, Building A – The Essential Manual (Shakespeare)
Dune Buggy Files (Hale)
Dune Buggy Handbook (Hale)
Edward Turner: The Man Behind The Motorcycles (Clew)
Fast Ladies – Female Racing Drivers 1888 to 1970 (Bouzanquet)
Fiat & Abarth 124 Spider & Coupé (Tipler)
Fiat & Abarth 500 & 600 2nd Edition (Bobbitt)
Fiats, Great Small (Ward)
Fine Art Of The Motorcycle Engine, The (Peirce)
Ford F100/F150 Pick-up 1948-1996 (Ackerson)
Ford F150 Pick-up 1997-2005 (Ackerson)
Ford GT – Then, And Now (Streather)
Ford GT40 (Legate)
Ford In Miniature (Olson)
Ford Model Y (Roberts)
Ford Thunderbird From 1954, The Book Of The (Long)
Formula 5000 Motor Racing, Back then ... and back now (Lawson)
Forza Minardi! (Vigar)
Funky Mopeds (Skelton)
Gentleman Jack (Gauld)
GM In Miniature (Olson)
GT – The World's Best GT Cars 1953-73 (Dawson)
Hillclimbing & Sprinting – The Essential Manual (Short & Wilkinson)
Honda NSX (Long)
Intermeccanica – The Story of the Prancing Bull (McCredie & Reisner)
Jaguar, The Rise Of (Price)
Jaguar XJ-S (Long)
Jeep CJ (Ackerson)
Jeep Wrangler (Ackerson)
John Chatham – 'Mr Big Healey' – The Official Biography (Burr)
Karmann-Ghia Coupé & Convertible (Bobbitt)
Lamborghini Miura Bible, The (Sackey)
Lambretta Bible, The (Davies)
Lancia 037 (Collins)
Lancia Delta HF Integrale (Blaettel & Wagner)
Land Rover, The Half-ton Military (Cook)
Laverda Twins & Triples Bible 1968-1986 (Falloon)
Lea-Francis Story, The (Price)
Lexus Story, The (Long)
Little book of smart, the New Edition (Jackson)
Lola – The Illustrated History (1957-1977) (Starkey)
Lola – All The Sports Racing & Single-seater Racing Cars 1978-1997 (Starkey)
Lola T70 – The Racing History & Individual Chassis Record 4th Edition (Starkey)
Lotus 49 (Oliver)
Marketingmobiles, The Wonderful Wacky World Of (Hale)
Mazda MX-5/Miata 1.6 Enthusiast's Workshop Manual (Grainger & Shoemark)
Mazda MX-5/Miata 1.8 Enthusiast's Workshop Manual (Grainger & Shoemark)
Mazda MX-5 Miata: The Book Of The World's Favourite Sportscar (Long)
Mazda MX-5 Miata Roadster (Long)
Maximum Mini (Booij)
MGA (Price Williams)
MGB & MGB GT– Expert Guide (Auto-doc Series) (Williams)
MGB Electrical Systems Updated & Revised Edition (Astley)
Micro Caravans (Jenkinson)
Micro Trucks (Mort)
Microcars At Large! (Quellin)
Mini Cooper – The Real Thing! (Tipler)
Mitsubishi Lancer Evo, The Road Car & WRC Story (Long)
Montlhéry, The Story Of The Paris Autodrome (Boddy)
Morgan Maverick (Lawrence)
Morris Minor, 60 Years On The Road (Newell)
Moto Guzzi Sport & Le Mans Bible, The (Falloon)
Motor Movies – The Posters! (Veysey)
Motor Racing – Reflections Of A Lost Era (Carter)
Motorcycle Apprentice (Cakebread)
Motorcycle Road & Racing Chassis Designs (Noakes)
Motorhomes, The Illustrated History (Jenkinson)
Motorsport In colour, 1950s (Wainwright)
Nissan 300ZX & 350Z – The Z-Car Story (Long)
Nissan GT-R Supercar: Born to race (Gorodji)
Off-Road Giants! – Heroes of 1960s Motorcycle Sport (Westlake)
Pass The Theory And Practical Driving Tests (Gibson & Hoole)
Peking To Paris 2007 (Young)
Plastic Toy Cars Of The 1950s & 1960s (Ralston)
Pontiac Firebird (Cranswick)
Porsche Boxster (Long)
Porsche 356 (2nd Edition) (Long)
Porsche 908 (Födisch, Neßhöver, Roßbach, Schwarz & Roßbach)
Porsche 911 Carrera – The Last Of The Evolution (Corlett)
Porsche 911R, RS & RSR, 4th Edition (Starkey)
Porsche 911 – The Definitive History 1963-1971 (Long)
Porsche 911 – The Definitive History 1971-1977 (Long)
Porsche 911 – The Definitive History 1977-1987 (Long)
Porsche 911 – The Definitive History 1987-1997 (Long)
Porsche 911 – The Definitive History 1997-2004 (Long)
Porsche 911SC 'Super Carrera' – The Essential Companion (Streather)
Porsche 914 & 914-6: The Definitive History Of The Road & Competition Cars (Long)
Porsche 924 (Long)
Porsche 928 (Long)
Porsche 944 (Long)
Porsche 964, 993 & 996 Data Plate Code Breaker (Streather)
Porsche 993 'King Of Porsche' – The Essential Companion (Streather)
Porsche 996 'Supreme Porsche' – The Essential Companion (Streather)
Porsche Racing Cars – 1953 To 1975 (Long)
Porsche Racing Cars – 1976 To 2005 (Long)
Porsche – The Rally Story (Meredith)
Porsche: Three Generations Of Genius (Meredith)
RAC Rally Action! (Gardiner)
Rallye Sport Fords: The Inside Story (Moreton)
Redman, Jim – 6 Times World Motorcycle Champion: The Autobiography (Redman)
Rolls-Royce Silver Shadow/Bentley T Series Corniche & Camargue Revised & Enlarged Edition (Bobbitt)
Rolls-Royce Silver Spirit, Silver Spur & Bentley Mulsanne 2nd Edition (Bobbitt)
Russian Motor Vehicles (Kelly)
RX-7 – Mazda's Rotary Engine Sportscar (Updated & Revised New Edition) (Long)
Scooters & Microcars, The A-Z Of Popular (Dan)
Scooter Lifestyle (Grainger)
Singer Story: Cars, Commercial Vehicles, Bicycles & Motorcycle (Atkinson)
SM – Citroën's Maserati-engined Supercar (Long & Claverol)
Speedway – Motor Racing's Ghost Tracks (Collins & Ireland)
Subaru Impreza: The Road Car And WRC Story (Long)
Supercar, How To Build your own (Thompson)
Tales from the Toolbox (Oliver)
Taxi! The Story Of The 'London' Taxicab (Bobbitt)
Tinplate Toy Cars Of The 1950s & 1960s (Ralston)
Toleman Story, The (Hilton)
Toyota Celica & Supra, The Book Of Toyota's Sports Coupés (Long)
Toyota MR2 Coupés & Spyders (Long)
Triumph Bonneville!, Save the – The inside story of the Meriden workers' co-op (Rosamond)
Triumph Motorcycles & The Meriden Factory (Hancox)
Triumph Speed Twin & Thunderbird Bible (Woolridge)
Triumph Tiger Cub Bible (Estall)
Triumph Trophy Bible (Woolridge)
Triumph TR6 (Kimberley)
Unraced (Collins)
Velocette Motorcycles – MSS To Thruxton Updated & Revised (Burris)
Virgil Exner – Visioneer: The Official Biography Of Virgil M Exner Designer Extraordinaire (Grist)
Volkswagen Bus Book, The (Bobbitt)
Volkswagen Bus Or Van To Camper, How To Convert (Porter)
Volkswagens Of The World (Glen)
VW Beetle Cabriolet (Bobbitt)
VW Beetle – The Car Of The 20th Century (Copping)
VW Bus – 40 Years Of Splitties, Bays & Wedges (Copping)
VW Bus Book, The (Bobbitt)
VW Golf: Five Generations Of Fun (Copping & Cservenka)
VW – The Air-cooled Era (Copping)
VW T5 Camper Conversion Manual (Porter)
VW Campers (Copping)
Works Minis, The Last (Purves & Brenchley)
Works Rally Mechanic (Moylan)

From Veloce Publishing's new imprints:

Battle Cry!
Soviet General & field rank officer uniforms: 1955 to 1991 (Streather)

Hubble & Hattie
Winston ... the dog who loved me (Klute)

www.veloce.co.uk

First published in June 2009 by Veloce Publishing Limited, 33 Trinity Street, Dorchester DT1 1TT, England. Fax 01305 268864/e-mail info@veloce.co.uk/web www.veloce.co.uk or www.velocebooks.com.
ISBN: 978-1-84584-183-6 UPC: 636847041830

Readers with ideas for automotive books, or books on other transport or related hobby subjects, are invited to write to the editorial director of Veloce Publishing at the above address.
British Library Cataloguing in Publication Data – A catalogue record for this book is available from the British Library. Typesetting, design and page make-up all by Veloce Publishing Ltd on Apple Mac. Printed in India by Replika Press.

Mini

Cooper

Graham Robson

Contents

Foreword

What is a rally? Today's events, for sure, are completely different from those of a hundred or even fifty years ago. What was once a test of reliability is now a test of speed and strength. What was once a long-distance trial is now a series of short-distance races.

In the beginning, rallying was all about using standard cars in long-distance road events, but by the 1950s the events were toughening up. Routes became rougher, target speeds were raised, point-to-point speed tests on special stages were introduced, and high performance machines were needed to ensure victory.

Starting in the late 1950s, too, teams started to develop extra-special versions of standard cars, which were built in small numbers, and meant only to go rallying, or motor racing. These were the 'homologation specials' which now dominate the sport. The first of these, no question, was the Austin-Healey 3000, the Mini Cooper followed soon afterwards, and the latest is any one of the ten-off World Rally Cars which we see on our TV screens, or on the special stages of the world.

Although rally regulations changed persistently over the years, the two most important events were four-wheel-drive

being authorised from 1979, and the 'World Rally Car' formula (which required only 20 identical cars to be produced to gain homologation) being adopted in 1997. At all times, however, successful rally cars have needed to blend high performance with strength and reliability.

Unlike Grand Prix cars, they have needed to be built so that major repairs could be carried out at the side of the road, in the dark, sometimes in freezing cold, and sometimes in blazing temperatures.

Over the years, some cars became dominant, only to be eclipsed when new and more advanced rivals appeared. New cars appeared almost every year, but dramatically better machines appeared less often. From time to time, rally enthusiasts would be astonished by a new model, and it was on occasions like that when a new rallying landmark was set.

So, which were the most important new cars to appear in the last half century? What is it that made them special, at the time? In some cases it was perfectly obvious – Lancia's Stratos was the first-ever purpose-built rally car, the Audi Quattro was the first rally-winning four-wheel-drive car, and the Toyota Celica GT4 was the first rally-winning four-wheel-drive Group A car to come from Japan.

But what about BMC's Mini Coopers? Or the amazing Ford Escorts? Or the Fiat 131 Abarth? Or the Lancia Delta Integrale? Or, of course, the Subaru Impreza? All of them had something unique to offer, at the time, in comparison with their competitors. Because they offered something different, and raised rallying's standards even further, they were true Rally Giants.

To a rallying petrol-head like me, it would have been easy to choose twenty, thirty or even more rally cars which have made a difference to the sport. However, I have had to be brutal, and cull my list to the very minimum. Listed here in chronological order, these are the 'Rally Giants' cars I have picked out, to tell the on-going story of world-class rallying in the last fifty years:

Car	Period used as a works car
Austin-Healey 3000	1959-1965
Saab 96 and V4	1960-1976
Mini Cooper/Cooper S	1962-1970
Ford Escort Mk I	1968-1975
Lancia Stratos	1974-1981
Ford Escort RS1800	1975-1981
Fiat 131 Abarth	1976-1981
Audi Quattro and S1	1981-1986
Peugeot 205T16	1984-1986
Lancia Delta 4x4/Integrale	1987-1993
Toyota Celica GT4	1988-1995
Ford Escort RS Cosworth/WRC	1993-1998
Mitsubishi Lancer Evo	1995-2001
Subaru Impreza Turbo/WRC	1993-2006
Peugeot 206WRC	1999-2003
Ford Focus WRC	1999-2005

There is so much to know, to tell, and to enjoy about each of these cars that I plan to devote a compact book to each one. And to make sure that one can be compared with another, I intend to keep the same format for each volume.

Graham Robson

Introduction & acknowledgements

In the 1960s, tens of thousands of enthusiasts began their motorsport careers inside the cabin of a Mini Cooper. Almost all of them fell in love with the car, either as drivers, or (in rallying) as co-driver/navigators, and never lost their affection for these amazing little machines.

Because the Mini Cooper was so outstanding in so many ways, and because BMC made sure that it became a very specialised competition car, it fell easily into the definition of a 'Rally Giant' – for without it, rallying – in particular European rallying – might have evolved in a different, more cumbersome, and altogether less exhilarating way. By comparison with any previous European rally car, the Mini Cooper was so much more effective than its specification promised it would be.

Now that the original generation of Mini has reached its fiftieth birthday, and any number of competitors were launched, grew up, and failed to match its qualities, millions of enthusiasts realise just what an important new car it actually was. Front-wheel-drive was one thing, small size was another, and superb handling was a different factor – but before Alec Issigonis' engineering team evolved the original Mini, such a beguiling combination of virtues had never before been achieved.

When race car constructor John Cooper inspired the birth of the Mini Coopers – really he had circuit racing in mind, but it wasn't long before the rallying fraternity realised just what potential he was unlocking for it too – he produced a car which had no all-round peers. Other cars handled well (but none ever handled better), others were certainly faster in a straight line, and others were perhaps more sturdy on loose-surface events, but none had the same combination of virtues.

By the time it matured, the Mini Cooper S had become one of the world's greatest rally cars, and it was only the appearance of the even more outstanding Ford Escort which saw it eventually matched. Not that the development of this little car was easy, or predictable. In the early days (pre-Mini Cooper, that is) the package was definitely under-powered and fragile, while the original Mini Coopers were still demonstrably making much out of frighteningly little, in a rather fingers-crossed manner. It was only when the definitive engine – the now world-famous S-Type – came along in 1963, and Abingdon learned how to make the little car very strong for specific duties, that all was well.

The Mini Cooper's career developed in several phases, each logically progressing from one to the next. Even so, it took several frustrating years – effectively from 1959 to 1964 – for the 'good idea' to become mature. The first Mini (the 848cc-engined variety, that is) was effectively forced upon Abingdon because BMC bosses wanted to see one of their smallest cars performing with honour, but it was always hopelessly under-powered, and was a real 'bottom-dragger' which often battered itself into retirement on loose-surface events.

The Mini Cooper which followed in 1962-1963 was an altogether better proposition. Not only did it have a much more powerful little engine, built close to the class capacity limit, but the disc brakes, though tiny, were a real improvement on the original drums. Furthermore, Abingdon was learning to add 'beef' to the chassis, and the 'works' cars soon proved their pace, especially on loose surfaces.

Complete with its much more specialised engine – a bigger bore/altogether more tuneable derivative of the original A-Series – the Mini Cooper S which followed also had bigger and better wheels and tyres, and was a much sturdier example than before. Once two different engine sizes – 970cc and 1275cc – became available, there seemed to be a Mini for almost all occasions.

For the next five years – 1964 to 1968 – the Mini Cooper S, particularly the 'works' variety, was formidable beyond all expectations – so much so that in many back-to-back conditions it could match the performance of its stable-mate, the Austin-Healey 3000. The only limits to its development were those of its front-wheel-drive traction and durability, and those of the engine itself. With the eight-port cylinder heads, and fuel-injection, more power, torque and straight line speed could still be achieved, but in the end the front tyres struggled for traction, and the chassis for balance.

If the new owner, British Leyland, had backed further work, instead of demanding victory from every outing (which was quite unreasonable), the Mini Cooper S might have gained even more honours, but by 1969 the glory days were really all over. It's only now, forty years on, that some of us realize just what an outstanding job it had always done.

Acknowledgements

Amazingly, when I settled down to write this book, I was sure that I already had all the necessary facts and images to hand. I was wrong. Accordingly, I needed a lot of help from other Mini Cooper specialists to make this a complete package.

Over the years, many have helped, and many continue to do so. When I recall that I first rallied in a Mini in 1960, first visited Abingdon in 1962, and have met the most amazing personalities, managers, historians and enthusiasts during the life time of the Mini, the miracle is that I even have space to thank them all.

In particular, it was Stuart Turner, Peter Browning, Bill Price and Basil Wales who led me behind the scenes so often. Not forgetting, of course, John Cooper, Ginger Devlin, Daniel Richmond and Jack Daniels …

Top mechanics like Doug Watts, Robin Vokins and Bryan Moylan explained much of the engineering. Star 'works' competitors like the 'Famous Five' [Pat Moss, Rauno Aaltonen, Tony Fall, Paddy Hopkirk and Timo Makinen], along with Paul Easter, the late and much-missed Henry Liddon, and Mike Wood all provided much information about the way in which BMC went rallying.

When it came to gathering and choosing illustrations for this book, I not only drew on my own archive, but also gained permission to use some invaluable images from MINI, the BMW-owned subsidiary which appreciates the heritage that it inherited when it was developing the model range. Peter Browning and Bill Price dug deep into their precious stocks, while Basil Wales added to the them, and I should mention that it was also Basil who led me gently through the various homologation papers.

Other invaluable information came from the BP Archive (BP now owns Castrol, which supported the 'works' Minis in the 1960s), from Bryan Moylan, and from Robert and Lesley Young of the Mini Cooper Register.

In closing, I want to repeat, once again, that none of we so-called historians could possibly do a competent job connected with Mini Coopers if Peter Browning and Bill Price had not already laid the foundations. Without them, the depths of the complex subject of re-born rally cars, cloned identities and outright fakery might still be unclear.

They, and those already mentioned above, have made the compilation of this latest volume in the Rally Giants series even more enjoyable than expected.

Graham Robson

Visit Veloce on the web – www.veloce.co.uk
Details of all books in print • Special offers • New book news • Gift vouchers • Forum

8

The car and the team

Inspiration

By 1960, the British Motor Corporation (BMC) had built up a formidable motorsport operation, based at the MG assembly plant at Abingdon, a few miles south of Oxford. Managed by Marcus Chambers, 'Comps' had developed from a very amateurish 'good chaps' team of 1955 into a very professional outfit. Having assessed every car in the sprawling BMC empire, the team had begun to concentrate on the Austin-Healey 3000 and MGA sports cars as front-line models, while starting development work on the new-fangled front-wheel-drive Minis which had been launched in 1959.

Although BMC would have loved to start winning races and rallies with the new Mini, which handled magnificently, here was a car which was let down by its lack of power (34bhp from 848cc was a derisory figure, after all …), limited

performance and its initial lack of reliability. There was also the worrying fact that no-one in the team – management, technicians or rally drivers – seemed to like the car.

As ever, it was that wise owl, Marcus Chambers, who put his finger on the problem. As he later wrote in the book *BMC Competitions Department Secrets*:

"A Mini 850 was delivered … It stayed in the car park for several days, nobody rushed to drive it. Indeed, Dougie Watts recalled that one lunchtime he needed to pop into town, and looked around for a car. Dougie walked over to the Mini … and then changed his mind. He took a Healey instead …"

Nevertheless, with image-building in mind, top management insisted that the 850 Mini should be developed, and used in motorsport wherever possible. Yet with only 848cc, it was not remotely likely to be turned into a winner – especially as it found itself in the same class as the recently-launched Saab 96, whose lead driver, the amazingly talented Erik Carlsson added to the problem.

Because FIA homologation rules meant that the single-SU carburettor and cast manifolds had to be retained, even though Weslake (and later Don Moore) modified heads could be employed, it was difficult to extract much more than 50bhp from the engine, but this was often enough to chew up oil seals and clutches. With tiny Dunlop racing tyres fitted to standard wheels on race circuits, it was soon obvious that the front wheels were not strong enough, and

Alec Issigonis conceived the original Mini in 1957, and wouldn't have known what a great little competition car he was about to unleash.

could crack up around the studs, and this duly happened in full view of the public in the 750 Motor Club's Six-Hour Relay race of 1960!

The first 'works' rally entry was by Marcus Chambers (a large man in a small car!) in the Norwegian Viking Rally of 1959, where it finished 51st, the first home win was by Pat Moss/Stuart Turner in the Knowldale CC Mini Miglia Rally (an event where pinpoint navigation was more important than car performance), and it took time even to gain class wins at international level.

The real inspiration, though, came from racing car constructor John Cooper, who not only got hold of an early Mini 850 – and found that several of his contemporaries, and the race drivers he hired, were impressed –

Every picture tells the story. In 1961 when the Mini Cooper was announced, BMC posed this car alongside the Cooper-BMC Formula Junior car, which used the same type of A-Series engine.

but also that larger versions of the engine (948cc power units were used in the Austin-Healey/ Sprite of the period) could be super-tuned.

It wasn't long before Cooper's first BMC-powered single-seater Formula Junior car was put on sale, after which he began developing a special version of the Mini: initially he proposed to sell conversions, as a private venture, but as everyone now knows, a lot

John Cooper started by building rear-engined race cars, but inspired the birth of the very first Mini Cooper of 1961.

of lobbying with Alec Issigonis and BMC managing director Sir George Harriman led to the launch of the Mini Cooper road car. Part of the deal which encompassed Cooper's name being used was that his company should be paid £2 per car – which must have been the biggest royalty bargain that BMC ever had.

The Mini Cooper's importance in rallying – and its home ground

When the Mini Cooper was launched in 1961, almost all British rallies were still of the overnight/navigational/twisty roads type, where nimble fast cars, preferably of small dimensions, were much more suitable than other types, and where the navigator (not, in those days, merely a co-driver) was a very important part of the team.

Until 1961, sports cars like the Austin-Healey Sprite and the Triumph TR3A were very popular and very successful in British rallying, and, if specific event regulations allowed, modified cars like big-engined Ford Anglias and 850 Minis were also making their mark. The 850 Mini, however, was not always fast enough to be competitive.

The very first Mini Coopers (this was a Morris-badged version) were introduced in 1961, looking almost identical to the Mini 850 of the day, and still wearing cross-ply tyres.

Here was a subtle piece of what the advertising industry would call 'product placement.' That is, an original Mini Cooper of 1961-1962, the model girls are professionals, but the helmeted race driver is Bruce McLaren, who was John Cooper's leading GP pilot at this stage.

The original 997cc Mini Cooper changed all that. It was significantly faster 'in the lanes' than its rivals, though bitter (and expensive) experience soon showed that it needed to be made much stronger to be competitive in the new breed of loose-surface/special-stage rallies which were springing up all around the country. Even so, on events like the Circuit of Ireland, where tests were usually located on tarmac roads, it was instantly competitive.

Once the Mini Cooper had been made more reliable on rough and tough events, its real importance in British rallies was that it gave all BMC enthusiasts and devotees a real alternative to using the Austin A35s, the Morris Minor 1000s, and the Austin-Healey Sprite/MG Midget-

types which they had previously favoured. It had the sort of handling that made all other cars seem clumsy, it was so small that somehow it made roads and tracks seem wider, while on low-friction surfaces such as snow, ice and muddy tracks, it usually had more traction, and could therefore go faster, than all its rivals.

BMC, too, was anxious to build up its 'tuning shop' business with private owners, and Abingdon (later Special Tuning, as a separate operation) immediately found a big demand for material to fit to Mini Coopers. Within two years of its launch, of course, the first of the Mini Cooper S-types also arrived, and both BMC and private owners began to concentrate on the cars, to the exclusion of most other machines.

Facing up to rival cars

This was the competition with which the Mini Cooper, and later the Mini Cooper S, was faced on the international rally scene in the 1960s:

Ford Cortina GT and Lotus-Cortina – front-engine/rear-drive. GT used regularly from 1963, Lotus-Cortina regularly used from 1965. Light but well-balanced, gradually developed, strengthened and made more reliable with the passing years. Lacking in traction on loose and icy/snow surfaces, but with a large operating budget, super-star drivers, and Ford's great determination to win. Soon succeeded by:

Ford Escort Twin-Cam – front-engine/rear-drive. Arrived in 1968, when the Mini Cooper S was at its peak, and soon came to establish dominance. With Lotus-Cortina running gear, but even faster and more durable. Also lacking

When the Mini Cooper S was coming to the fore, front-wheel-drive Saabs, especially when driven by Erik Carlsson, were among the cars which had to be beaten. This was Erik on top of the Turini on the 1964 Monte Carlo rally. (Reproduced from the BP/Castrol Archive)

in traction on loose/ice/snow, but backed by Ford's great determination. The Escort would go on to have a 13-year career at the top.

Porsche 911 – rear-engine/rear-drive. A carefully-engineered sports coupé, first used in 1965. Already available in a 160bhp/2.0-litre version at that time with much more to come. Superb traction. Vic Elford would win the European Championship in 1967, and the Monte Carlo Rally in 1968: Björn Waldegård would then win two Montes in larger-engined cars. There was always much more potential in this car than Porsche ever employed, though it was gradually realised in later years. Rivals were relieved that Porsche chose to concentrate on circuit racing.

Alpine-Renault A110 – rear-engine/rear-drive. First used in 1964. Tubular back-bone chassis frame, and ultra-light GRP bodyshell. Available with a 1.3-litre engine from 1965, with more to come – after the Mini years it would be enlarged to 1.8 litres. Superb traction. Still fragile in the mid-1960s, not yet a winner, but sure to be so when reliability was gained.

Lancia Fulvia HF – front-engine/front-drive. First used in 1966. A 1.2 litre, then 1.3 litre, at this time, but with 1.6 litre/5-speed transmission set to come in 1968/1969 (just after the Mini's 'golden years') – and superb traction. Not yet powerful enough to win everywhere, but a seemingly enormous budget made up for much of that. Lancia, it seemed, would pay handsomely for success.

Saab 96, Sport and V4 – front-engine/front-drive. First used (as Saab 96) in 1960, as V4 in 1967. Rock-solid in both guises, and developed carefully with loose-surface stages in mind. Under-powered as 96/Sport with original three-cylinder two stroke, but more brawny as the V4 with Ford-Germany 1.5-litre four-stroke engine in 1967: more potential for 1.7 litres to follow. Superb traction. Powerful enough to win on snow/ice, and in some forestry events, but reaching its limits in the late 1960s.

Homologation – meeting the rules

When applying for sporting recognition ('homologation') for its cars, BMC was at least as open, or as honest, as any of its rivals when it came to getting cars into motorsport as soon as possible. In every case – whether it be 997cc Mini Cooper, 970S, 1071S, 1275S or Mini-Clubman 1275GT – the model was originally homologated into Group 2, which meant that the authorities had to accept that 1000 such cars had already been manufactured within a year.

Although BMC's managing director, Sir George Harriman, had once doubted the possibility of BMC even selling a total of one thousand Mini Coopers, he was soon proved wrong, for there never seemed to be any lack of demand from the general public. Accordingly, and except that BMC pushed through the homologation process just as soon as it could, homologation of all these cars was very genuinely achieved.

Although this was a period when BMC was manufacturing less-specialised Minis (mostly with 34bhp/848cc engines) on two massive sites – one at Longbridge near Birmingham (the historic 'Austin' factory), the other at Cowley, near Oxford (the 'Morris' factory) – each and every Mini Cooper, whether carrying an 'Austin' or a 'Morris' badge, was always assembled at Longbridge. Because it was still BMC policy to produce cars for both original (and historic) arms of its dealer chain – Austin and Morris – naturally the Mini Cooper had to be made available as an 'Austin' or as a 'Morris,' and at no time were there any technical differences between the two. Homologation papers referred to both brands on the same piece of paper. The FIA, at least, recognised this commercial reality, so when the time came to have the cars approved, the niceties of which cars had what badge on the bonnet, steering wheel and boot lid were ignored.

[As far as Abingdon was concerned, this occasionally led to confusion. There are authenticated cases, backed up with photographs, and by comments in the sporting media, where a particular 'works' car changed its badging during its career, and cars were also known to start events (by mistake!) with a mixture of Austin and Morris identification on grilles, badges and the steering-wheel boss!]

Mini Coopers – how many were made?

As with almost everything connected with BMC and British Leyland, getting at true, firm, unarguable facts on production figures is difficult. In addition, we must not forget the fact that the 'Mini Cooper' badge was revived in the 1990s, though those cars were not directly linked to the 'classic' Mini Coopers of the 1961-1971 period. However, these are two related sets of figures which refer to the 1961-1971 generation, issued at different times by BMIHT archivists, which more or less put things straight:

Total production:

Model	Number produced
Mini Cooper 997cc	24,860
Mini Cooper 998cc MkI	39,364
Mini Cooper 998cc MkII	16,396
Mini Cooper S 970cc	963
Mini Cooper S 1071cc	4031
Mini Cooper S 1275cc MkI	14,313
Mini Cooper S 1275cc MkII	6329
Mini Cooper S 1275cc MkIII	**19,511

**This figure includes cars sold to Innocenti for re-invention as Innocenti types!

Annual production:

Year	Mini Cooper (997cc & 998cc)	Mini Cooper S (MkI & MkII)	Mini Cooper S (MkIII)
1961	1644	-	-
1962	13,916	-	-
1963	9526	1590	-
1964	9229	5679	-
1965	8269	4950	-
1966	14,130	4011	-
1967	13,102	3896	-
1968	14,667	3701	-
1969	13,978	3111	-
1970	-	-	9436
1971	-	-	10,075

In almost every case, the sale of fully built-up 'Austin' and 'Morris'-types was split into approximately a 50 per cent market share of each model.

Because the Mini Cooper (and even the more specialised Mini Cooper S, in later years) was so very closely based on the normal mass-market Mini, the cars were always put together on the same assembly lines at Longbridge. Indeed, until the moment at which the different grille and badging (and, of course, the different engine/transmission/front suspension assembly) was applied, it was only the addition of the contrasting roof panel colour which made it clearly possible to tell the shells apart.

The only case where homologation regulations were pushed to the limit was with the 970S, where production of the special short-stroke engine was slow in getting started, but where homologation was requested (and granted) only three months after launch in March 1964. It is doubtful if more than a handful of such cars had been built by that time and, as Stuart Turner later wrote in *Twice Lucky*: "During the year there was one particular showroom demonstrator that sales chief Lester Suffield arranged to be shipped regularly around Europe to convince the world that they were widely available ..."

In the hey-day of the 'works' Mini Cooper S, until 1966 there was never any need to look for Group 1 homologation. Then, when the 1966 Monte Carlo regulations were studied, it suddenly became essential that the 1275S should qualify. Happily, certain other manufacturers cheated, claiming (with feigned wide-eyed innocence) that their cars were being built in suitable quantities, BMC had only a minor problem, which was soon resolved.

As Peter Browning later confirmed: "What the Rally organisers did not realise was that successful rallying sells cars, and the year's production figure for the Mini Cooper S stood at just under 5000. By stepping up production just a little, 5047 identical cars were built within the specific 12 months ..."

This was the only special case, where one of the derivatives was also homologated as a Group 1 car – this being the Hydrolastically-suspended 1275S – so that it could compete in the 1966 Monte Carlo Rally, where Group 1 regulations were to be applied for the first (and, as it transpired, the only) time in the history of the event.

To achieve Group 1 homologation – in which, compared with Group 2, far fewer optional extras were authorised – no fewer than 5000 identical cars had to be manufactured, and as we now know, this was achieved.

By the end of 1965, of course, the Mini Cooper S had already won the Monte Carlo Rally twice. It can now be stated, quite categorically, that the Monegasque organisers applied the Group 1 rule to their event because they were convinced that the Mini Cooper S (and, by the way, the Ford Lotus-Cortina) could never qualify for Group 1 homologation. They were wrong.

As we now know, the 'works' team went on to dominate the 1966 Monte, but the organisers were so determined to get them out of contention that they applied an extremely dubious interpretation of headlamp operating regulations to disqualify the cars instead. This was one of only a few isolated occasions in which a 'Group 1' 'works' entry was made in an international rally.

Engineering features

Without the inbuilt genius of Alec Issigonis' original 848cc Mini-Minor, cars like the increasingly specialised Mini Cooper and Mini Cooper S models could never have been developed, for the design, development and manufacture of such a front-wheel-drive car would never have been justified. Apart from the original inventiveness, as far as motorsport was concerned, the real brilliance came in extracting so much power, so much reliability, and so much operational flexibility from a layout which was never intended to be the basis of a competition car. It is worth emphasising, yet again, that Alec Issigonis had originally laid out the first Mini as

being an ultra-cheap, ultra-small model, aimed at sweeping all European competition off the roads.

An analysis of engineering features, therefore, must be split into several sections – first of all, those which applied to all Minis of all types, and secondly, those which were then applied to the Mini Coopers themselves:

Unique at the time was the fact that the cars – all of them four-door saloons with two passenger doors – were incredibly compact (they were just ten-feet long), this partly being achieved by the use of a transversely-mounted engine, the gearbox under the engine, all allied to front-wheel-drive and tiny ten-inch diameter wheels. Other rally cars had used front-wheel-drive – currently, the Saab 93, soon to be replaced by the Saab 96, was the most important type – but such cars were invariably much larger, and much heavier than the new Mini.

This original BMC drawing, dating from the late 1950s, shows just how small the original 850 Mini actually was, and how very cramped the engine bay was, which enclosed the transversely-mounted A-Series power unit. In original form there was 34bhp available, but from 1964 road versions of the 1275S produced 76bhp, and fully-tuned race/rally cars sometimes had close to 130bhp.

A-Series engines

This famous little power unit, which became the cornerstone of all small BMC cars built from 1951 until the 1990s, was designed in the late 1940s, first launched in 1951 for the Austin A30 family car, and last seen on the very last of the 'classic' Minis manufactured in 1990. Because this four-cylinder/water-cooled power unit was originally designed purely as a mass production engine, with no pretensions to high performance, it had very basic engineering. Further, because machine tooling was installed with a view to building millions of cheap-to-manufacture 'peas-in-a-pod' engines, this unit had no advanced features – so, in the 1960s and 1970s, when the use of more powerful and highly developed power units was at its height, the miracle was that such potent little engines could actually be made.

Although all production line engines were afflicted with the use of cast-iron five-port cylinder heads (two inlet ports, three exhaust ports), and the original engine of 1951 was a 948cc unit, over the years it was made both smaller then larger. The major change of interior architecture came in 1963, for the S-type cylinder blocks, where the position of the cylinder barrels was shuffled around to allow larger cylinder bore dimensions to be used.

Over the years, therefore, this was the range of A–Series engine derivatives which went on sale:

Capacity	Bore x stroke (mm)	Originally used in	First seen	Comment
848cc	62.94 x 68.26	Mini 850	1959	Short stroke-version of 948cc engine
948cc	62.94 x 76.2	Austin A30	1951	Original type
970cc	70.64 x 61.91	Mini Cooper S	1964	Only used on Mini Cooper 970S
997cc	62.43 x 81.28	Mini Cooper	1961	Only used on Mini Cooper 997
998cc	64.59 x 76.2	Riley Elf/Wolseley Hornet	1963	Short-stroke version of 1098cc engine, always a mainstream unit.
1071cc	70.64 x 68.26	Mini Cooper S	1963	Only used on Mini Cooper 1071S
1098cc	64.59 x 83.73	Morris 1100	1962	Always a mainstream unit
1095cc	70.64 x 69.85	South African Minis	1971	Effectively a long-stroke version of the 1071cc engine
1275cc	70.64 x 81.33	Mini Cooper S	1964	Originally for 1275S, later re-engineered for 'mainstream' use

To make all this possible, what engineers called the 'packaging' was as tight as humanly possible, and the engine water cooling radiator was installed on the left side limits of the engine bay, mounted up to a slatted inner wheel-arch panel: controversy about the name of that panel is easily deflected, for that is what the BMC engineers always called this location.

All four wheels were independently suspended by what was effectively a twin wishbone front end, and with trailing arms at the rear. All cars used rubber cone suspension (Alec Issigonis had originally wanted to use Hydrolastic units, but these were both too costly, and not finally developed, so would not appear until 1964), allied to ten-inch diameter road wheels, 5.20x10in, cross-ply tyres, and seven-inch diameter drum brakes. Rack-and-pinion steering was also used; it was mounted behind the engine/transmission location, was very difficult to change in a hurry, and was one of the features about which 'works' rally mechanics could – and did – grumble in years to come.

A feature of the very short overall length was that something approaching a 'sit-up-and-beg' driving position was imposed, the steering column was more vertical than that of conventional cars, and on the original 850s the gearlever was a rather long and flexible 'wand' which protruded from the toe board. Just one small (5½ gallon) fuel tank was included, all exposed to view in the small luggage boot at the rear.

This study explains why the Achilles heel of all high-powered Mini Cooper S-types was the transmission, for all the gears were crammed into this single casting, under the engine block itself. Because of homologation restrictions, there was no way that BMC could alter this casting, without building 5000 special cars – which it never did.

This was the wooden mock-up of the very first Mini, dating from 1957. At the time there was no thought of turning the car into a competition machine.

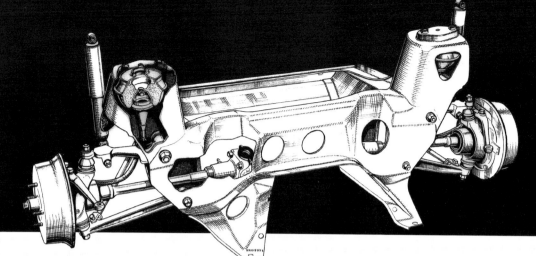

Each and every classic Mini was built around this massive front sub-frame, which supported the engine, transmission, suspension and steering units. This was the original 850 type, with drum brakes, but Mini Cooper and Mini Cooper S-types were very similar.

Alec Issigonis

Born in Smyrna, Greece, in 1906, of a Greek father and a German mother, Alec Issigonis was brought to Europe after the family fled the consequences of the Greco-Turkish war in 1922, and shortly became British citizens. Having studied in England at Battersea Polytechnic, Issigonis then worked for a company selling novel motorcar transmission systems, before joining the engineering design offices of Humber Ltd (which did all the engineering for Hillman too) in 1934.

Moving south to join Morris Motors, at Cowley, in 1936, he soon became involved in chassis and suspension work, during the Second World War he dabbled in all manner of military oddities, and eventually saw his first 'whole-car' exercise, the Morris Minor, launched in 1948. Not only did the Minor have excellent handling, it also used rack-and-pinion steering, so Issigonis's reputation was made for ever.

Four years later, having made a front-wheel-drive Minor, and seen it rejected by his new bosses at BMC, Issigonis left to join Alvis in Coventry, where he designed an ambitious new model, the TA350, which was cancelled before it could reach production. Tempted back to BMC at the end of 1955, at Chairman Sir Leonard Lord's behest, he set up a small, secretive, long-term research

department, and it was there in 1957 that the original Mini – ADO 15 – was born. Announced in 1959, and gleefully promoted by BMC, it was a great success, and Issigonis therefore became the all-seeing, all-powerful guru at BMC – a position he was to hold until 1968.

Having been swept into the mainstream of engineering work at BMC, Issigonis eventually became Technical Director, and joined the board. Arrogant, single-minded, and sure of his own skills, he rarely listened to anyone about the practicalities of his new designs, which included the 1100 (another major success), the 1800 (by no means as fast selling), and the Maxi which followed in 1969. All had transversely-mounted engines, front-wheel-drive and Hydrolastic suspension.

Although he had started work on a complete Mini replacement – the '9X' project – by the time Leyland merged with BMC to form British Leyland in 1968, that project was soon cancelled. Issigonis was briskly sidelined by the dominant Leyland management, and given the rather meaningless title of 'Director, Research and Development.' Little was achieved in his final years and he retired, embittered and largely ignored, in 1972.

After a long but rather solitary retirement (he never married), he died in Birmingham in 1988.

Before the end of 1960, longer-wheelbase estate car and panel van-types were also announced, and as the years passed by there would also be up-market (with different noses and tails) Riley and Wolseley-badged types, and the ruggedly simple open-topped Mini Moke 'roadster.'

The first of the Mini Coopers, about which this book is almost totally concerned, was announced in September 1961. Closely-based on the 850 of the period, and provided with 'Austin' and 'Morris' badges, these cars had long-stroke, 55bhp, 997cc engines, with twin semi-downdraught SU carburettors and sixteen-bladed cooling fans, a remote-control gear change (which was a great improvement), and 7.0in Lockheed front-wheel disc brakes, though cross-ply tyres and narrow (3.5in) rim wheels were still standard.

Jumping out of sequence, just a little, in January 1964 (UK – earlier in South Africa) the '997' Mini Cooper became the '998' Mini Cooper, with a change of A-Series engine. This isn't the place to describe all the ins-and-outs of BMC engine provisioning at the time, but the difference between the two engines was very significant, as this simple table shows:

Mini Cooper

Capacity	Bore x stroke (mm)	Power@RPM	Comment
997cc	62.43 x 81.28	55@6000	Only used in 997 Mini Cooper
998cc	64.6 x 76.2	55@5800	Became a standard size, though differently rated, and used in millions of other Minis.

Birth of the Mini

When Alec Issigonis (see profile on page 18) conceived the new front-wheel-drive Mini in 1957, he never intended it to become a successful competition car. In his master plan, this was to be an ultra-small, ultra-cheap, 'peoples' car which (he hoped) would sweep all other small family cars off the road. There were no plans for larger or higher performance engines, and no question of any performance raising options, either in the engine, transmission or chassis. This partly explains why the 'works' team at Abingdon originally had such a hard time making its new rally cars both reliable and versatile.

Original design work began in 1957, full approval for production on two sites – Longbridge (the existing 'Austin' factory) and Cowley (the 'Morris' plant) – came in mid-1958, and the new Austin and Mini-badged 848cc versions were launched simultaneously in August 1959.

What became affectionately known as the 'classic' Mini then had a phenomenally long, successful, but only marginally profitable life. Although well over 125,000 of all Mini Cooper-badged cars were produced between 1961 and 1971, this was only a small proportion (less than 2.5 per cent) of the 5.38 million Minis of all types which were produced between 1959 and 1990.

Once the Mini Cooper S was introduced, of course, the Mini Cooper was of no further relevance to race and rally enthusiasts. S-type engines could produce much more power, and were always preferred. Production of 998cc Mini Cooper road cars ended in 1969, and was never revived.

S-type and later improvements

Although the 1071S came first, and the 970S was only a strictly limited-edition car, the three derivatives – 970S, 1071S and 1275S – were effectively three sub-divisions of the same time. Their individual life-spans were:

970S	June 1964-April 1965
1071S	March 1963-August 1964
1275S	April 1964-June 1971

Compared with the Mini Cooper, the Mini Cooper S had a much more robust A-Series power unit, where the position of the cylinder barrel casting cores had been moved around to allow for bigger cylinder bores, allied to different cylinder head castings, and a sturdier cylinder block and crankshaft. Based on the same long-established A-Series layout, their differences were as follows:

Capacity	Bore x stroke (mm)	Power@RPM	Comment
970cc	70.6 x 61.91	65@6500	Unique to the 970S
1071cc	70.6 x 68.26	70@6200	Unique to the 1071S
1275cc	70.6 x 81.33*	76@5800	Later became a standard size, though differently rated, and used in millions of other BMC/British Leyland cars

*81.33mm is the officially quoted figure. That of the 997cc Mini Cooper was 81.28mm. The difference – 0.05mm, or 0.002in – is absolutely negligible. In Imperial measure, both are close enough to 3.20in, which is the good old-fashioned measure used by production engineers at Longbridge!

In addition to the engine changes, Mini Cooper S cars had enlarged front-wheel disc brakes, perforated wheels, 3.5in, or 4.5in rim widths, and 145x10in radial ply tyres.

From September 1964, all Mini saloons (including Cooper and Cooper S types) were given 'ride on water' Hydrolastic suspension instead of rubber cone springs – which meant that the 'works' team, and drivers, had a choice in the years which followed. The 'wet' system certainly gave a softer ride but, when used in modified form, opinions as to the most effective system were widely different.

The wider rim wheels became standard from late 1965 and, in connection with the re-homologation of the 1275S into Group 1 in January 1966, from that point the cars were always built with twin fuel tanks (doubling the capacity) and an engine oil cooler.

MkI cars gave way to MkII in October 1967, which was mechanically insignificant, though the front grille was enlarged, as was the rear window. During 1968 (it was a gradual change over, not accurately annotated), an all-synchromesh transmission took over from the unsynchronised first gear variety. MkII gave way to MkIII from March 1970 (which meant the use of concealed-hinge doors, and wind-up windows), while the last car of all was produced in June 1971. It is thought that a few of the final

BMC modified the Mini Cooper family in October 1967, calling them MkII models. Mechanically, there was little change, though the grille was slightly larger than before.

cars may have reverted to rubber cone suspension, though factory records are vague on this subject.

[The Mini Cooper 'brand' would be re-introduced in 1990, and the John Cooper business produced a 'Mini Cooper S' conversion of these cars – but neither belongs closely to the breed of cars described here.]

When BMW launched the new generation Mini Cooper S in the early 2000s, it made sure that the link with the past was emphasised. Incidentally, though new and old types both carry the magic lettering '33 EJB' in this study, neither is the real deal …

This head-on shot, with both cars showing the false but charismatic use of '33 EJB,' shows how much larger the re-born MINI Cooper S of the early 2000s was than the original S-type of the period 1959-2000.

Motorsport development – and improvements

Before beginning to survey the Mini Coopers in detail, it's worth noting that the original 850 Mini was introduced at the end of August 1959, while FIA Homologation was achieved less than a month later – on 17 September 1959. Forms 1047 (Austin) and 1048 (Morris) were very simple documents, with no performance options of any sort being listed.

Mini Cooper (used 1962 and 1963)

There were two reasons why the original Mini Cooper did not benefit from a great deal of development as a 'works' car in 'works' motorsport. First of all, it had such a brief career – effectively January 1962 to mid-1963 – and secondly, because work on its successor, the 1071S, was well under way by the end of 1962.

Work on the real ancestor of these cars – the 850 Mini – had concentrated on making the cars reliable, although much was also done to every aspect of the engineering. Work on engine development was ongoing and several companies or individuals were involved. Originally, Weslake (of Rye) consulted – up at Longbridge, BMC had an on-going contract with that company – but by 1960 Don Moore (of Cambridge) was favoured by the 'works' department at Abingdon. Later, Eddie Maher's development at Morris Engines, and John Cooper (for the Formula Junior race car programme) would also be involved, as was Daniel Richmond at Downton Engineering in Wiltshire. Transmission assemblies, gradually becoming more and more special, were supplied from Longbridge. By 1961, the build sheet for an 850 Mini encompassed at least 150 separate operations.

When the time came to develop the 997cc-engined Mini Cooper, development work built on what was already known about the 850. A typical build sheet would mention up to 300 items and procedures, all of which were carried out by the one fitter/mechanic who was building that car. By that time, Abingdon mechanics would also be building up their own engine. Then, front drive shafts, and drive shaft joints, were still standard, though stronger (and noisier!)

straight-cut gears had been adopted. Engines which used twin 1½in SU carburettors tended to produce about 70bhp at the flywheel – which would equate to perhaps 60bhp if measured on the rolling road, though this was not installed at Abingdon until a later date.

In addition to Geoff Mabbs' own car (in which Rauno Aaltonen suffered the fiery crash on the 1962 Monte Carlo), there were six 'works' cars – 737 ABL, 407 ARX, 977 ARX, 477 BBL, 17 CRX and 18 CRX.

The original homologation form quoted a choice of twin carburettors – 1¼in or 1½in SUs – along with two different sets of gearbox ratios (the standard set, and the wider-ratio 850 model set), along with four different final drive ratios – 3.44:1, 3.765:1 (standard), 4.133:1, 4.26:1 and 4.786:1.

From 11 April 1964, when the 998cc version of the car was approved, it carried the FIA Recognition number of 1298. Among the options, incidentally, was a 'High Traction Differential' – which we may assume is a different phrase for 'Limited Slip Differential.'

Among the authorised optional equipment were twin fuel tanks, totalling 45 litres (10 gallons), a sump guard, engine oil cooler, and a 'touring' camshaft with less extreme valve timing.

Some of these details would be carried over to the later Mini Cooper S types.

Mini Cooper 970S (used 1964, 1966 and 1967)

As far as rallying was concerned, the 970S was almost invisible. Originally engineered to be an ideal 'class car' in touring car racing, it was rarely useful to BMC's rally team, which was always looking for outright victories – for which the 1275S was more promising.

Looking down the lists, it seems that the 970S was used as a 'works' rally car on only three occasions – in the 1964 French Alpine, in the 1964 Tour de France (in which much motor racing was involved, and the 1.0-litre class was important), and in the 1966 Polish Rally – in each case where the regulations favoured a smaller-engined Mini Cooper, or where 'works' cars were entered in more than one group in the same event.

On one other famous occasion in 1967, more as racing cars than rally cars, two 970Ss were entered in the 84-Hour Marathon de la Route at the Nürburgring, where one car finished second overall. According to their registration numbers (if these can be trusted!), both had previously been used as 1275S rally cars …

Except that the 970S used a unique, short-stroke engine, visually, mechanically, and in terms of its build state and schedule, a 970S was almost entirely the same as the 1275S's which were being used at the time.

No dedicated 970S car was ever originally built as a rally car at Abingdon. However, where the regulations/handicaps suited Minis in a 1-litre class, the following normally 1275S-types were re-engined on special occasions: AJB 44B, AJB 66B, BJB 77B, GRX 5D, GRX 309D and LRX 830E – though most of them reverted to normal 1275S engines afterwards.

In all important respects, except for the engine itself, details of the 970S homologation followed those of the 1275S.

Mini Cooper 1071S (used 1963 and 1964)

Paddy Hopkirk's legendary victory in the 1964 Monte Carlo Rally was in a 1071S, which somehow makes people think that this particular model had a long and important career. In fact, the 1071's 'works' career was very short – from June 1963 to January 1964 inclusive! Because of this, there were only five 'works' 1071S rally cars: 8 EMO, 277 EBL, 33 EJB (the legendary Hopkirk/Monte car of 1964), 569 FMO and 570 FMO – two of these cars became 1275S-types later in their careers …

For that reason, the 1071S may be considered as an 'interim' works car, on which there was little time to carry out dedicated development work, though much of what was done was carried forward to the 1275S which followed.

Even at this time, the transmission was usually standard intermediate gear ratios, but wheel hub bearings had been replaced by Timken roller bearings. Paddy Hopkirk's Monte car used a near-standard cylinder head and a standard camshaft, which nevertheless had a 10.5:1 compression ratio, with standard intermittent gear ratios and a 4.1:1 final drive ratio.

When BMC announced the original Mini Cooper 1071S in 1963, it could only be identified from other Minis the 'S' badging on the nose, and by the use of radial ply tyres as standard. This was a Morris-based version (there was also an 'Austin'-type).

On other events a more extreme tune (11.0:1 compression, and a special camshaft) might be used – the result being that the best engines had up to 92bhp at the flywheel, perhaps 75bhp at the road wheels.

Details of the original 1071S homologation, achieved on 9 May 1963, included a choice of 1¼in or 1½in SU carburettors, 9.0:1 or 11.0:1 compression ratio pistons, two different sets of gear ratios, and three different final drive ratios. These were the transmission options:

Standard internal ratios: 3.2:1, 1.916:1, 1.357:1, 1.00:1
Optional internal ratios: 2.567:1, 1.78:1, 1.242:1, 1.00:1
Final drive ratios: 3.44:1, 3.765:1, 4.133:1

Fuel capacity was listed as 25 litres or 50 litres (therefore allowing twin tanks) while an alternative shape of tubular exhaust system was also illustrated.

Mini Cooper 1275S (used 1964 to 1970)

Because this was a Mini derivative which always seemed to be competitive, could win in many different conditions, and had a lusty engine, it was the 1275S which received most attention from the development team at Abingdon. First used in 1964, and last used (in Clubman-bodied shape) six years later in 1970, it was a winner for four years, and an oh-so-nearly winner until the very end of its career.

When the 1275S was re-homologated (in Group 1 guise) in January 1966, it was pointed out that more than 5000 cars had been counted between 7 December 1964 and 3 December 1965. All existing homologation details already quoted for early-type 970S, 1071S and 1275Ss were carried forward, plus:

Under Group 1: The available final drive ratios were 3.44:1 and 4.133:1.
Under Group 2: The available final drive ratios were 3.44, 3.765, 3.938, 4.133, 4.26 or 4.786:1.
Under Group 2: Internal gear ratios were quoted as 3.20, 1.916, 1.357, 1.00 and (reverse) 3.2:1
– or, optionally:
2.57, 1.72, 1.25, 1.00 and (reverse) 2.57.

In addition, a limited slip differential, heavy-duty Hydrolastic units, and 60-litre fuel tank were listed as options.

From 1964, much more engine and transmission development work was carried out at Abingdon than in earlier years, especially after a rolling road dynamometer had been installed. Engines produced more than 100bhp (flywheel)/80bhp+ (rolling road) from the start, and were improved slightly but significantly in the years which followed. With Downton-modified cylinder heads, and the well respected '648' camshaft available at once, there was not much more that could be achieved thereafter – not, that is, until alternative carburation and even an eight–port/cross-flow cylinder head became available.

1½in SU carburettors and ported standard inlet manifolds were used, though on the 1968 Monte twin prototype Weber carbs (which, as we shall see in the 'Competition story' section) were fitted to the standard manifolds and were worth about 7bhp.

Minis didn't only go rallying, but racing, too. Three 1275S-types (a Broadspeed car in the rear) at Silverstone in 1965.

Detail development for the next several years was on-going, though one sometimes had to look very carefully, and in almost forensic detail, to see when changes were introduced, some of them only where liberal event-by-event regulations allowed, and if the cars were running in the Group 3 (GT) or even the Group 6 (Prototype) categories. The following note some, but not all, of those:

1964: Aluminium doors, bonnet and boot lid panels were produced for Group 3 and Group 6 cars. Along with Perspex side and rear glass, these would find use on any number of non-homologated 'works' cars in the next six years.

A limited slip differential was made available (it was originally listed at £49.50), this being much more usable on the race track, rather than on rallies where the torque-steer characteristics were not as predictable.

1965: Wheel-arch extensions were fitted, to cover wide-rim wheels and fat tyres: Timo Makinen's 1965 Monte victory, in a Group 3 car, was achieved with the first of these.

1966: As an engine oil cooler, and twin fuel tanks (total capacity 11.0 gallons) were henceforth fitted to all 1275S road cars, these were speedily homologated at the beginning of the year, though not in time for the Monte Carlo Rally. The new Group 1 Homologation was listed under FIA Recognition 5028.

Hardy Spicer inner drive shaft joints took over from the original rubber variety in the Monte Carlo Rally, and were then standardised, for the remainder of the 1275S' career.

Even by the mid-1966s, 'works' racing 1275S-types demonstrated why tyre life and front-wheel-drive traction would eventually be a problem with the rally team. This was John Rhodes leading a team-mate in a Group 5 race at Brands Hatch.

Function before styling beauty – this is a typical fascia/instrument panel layout of a Mini Cooper S. Note the Heuer watches and the Halda Twinmaster in front of the co-driver, along with a windscreen washer bottle and a row of electrical fuses. The electrically-heated windscreen suggests that this is a Monte car.

This was the boot area of a 'works' 1071S, kitted out for the 1964 Monte Carlo rally. Note the twin fuel tanks.

In the 1960s, the 'works' Competitions Department at Abingdon was still low-tech, but full of resourceful and enthusiastic people. Minis and an MGB appear here, and by the looks of the studded tyres, this is definitely a pre-Monte Carlo shot, taken in January.

The preparation workshops at Abingdon could accommodate no more than about ten to twelve cars in very cramped conditions. This shot was taken in 1966, with (closest to the camera) GRX 195D being built up as a fully-tuned Group 2 example.

Driving this brand-new showroom standard Group 1 car, GRX 555D, Timo Makinen and Paul Easter demolished all opposition, to finish first in the 1966 Monte Carlo Rally. After a series of scandalous decisions by the scrutineers of the event, they were disqualified on trivial grounds concerning a headlamp infringement.

Not only did magnesium Minilite wheels look very attractive, they also saved a great deal of weight. Homologated for 1967, and used on most 'works' Minis after that, they sold in huge quantities to private owners, too.

Sweet revenge for the disqualifications of the 1966 Monte Carlo came a year later, when Rauno Aaltonen and Henry Liddon drove LBL 6D to outright victory in the 1967 event. Cast-magnesium Minilite wheels were used for the first time on a 'works' rally Mini.

By 1966 the engine bay of a Group 2 1275S was stuffed full of machinery. This car, caught at Abingdon while being built up, shows off the positioning of the engine oil cooler (behind the front grille), the strident air horns (mounted above the brake servo), and the fact that a Lucas dynamo (not an alternator) was still being used.

1967: Magnesium alloy (Minilite) road wheels were homologated from January – Rauno Aaltonen's Monte victory was achieved with these. They became standard equipment on 'works' cars.

A new eight-port cylinder head, allied to Lucas fuel-injection, was first seen on Group 5 race cars, and in non-homologated form in practice for the Tour de Corse. It would eventually be homologated into Group 2 as the final significant improvement to the 1275cc A-Series engine. It would certainly have been driven by Timo Makinen in Group 6 form in the 1967 RAC Rally, but this was the event cancelled one day before the start (due to a nationwide outbreak of bovine foot-and-mouth disease.

1968: Specially-developed prototype Weber carburettors (effectively single choke adaptations of the famous dual-choke DCOE-type), allied to the existing five-port cylinder head, were used, controversially, but quite legally, on the Monte Carlo Rally (third, fourth and fifth overall). These were not homologated nor (correctly as it transpired) did they need to be.

Additional front shock absorbers were added to give more control on Hydrolastic suspension cars.

5.5in-rim Minilite road wheels were used for the first time.

12in Minilite wheels were first used on the Group 5 John Cooper 'works' 1275S cars. Trials would eventually be carried out on 'works' rally cars, but were invariably unsuccessful, as the handling of the cars was only acceptable on smooth tarmac racing sections.

Here is an object lesson in packaging, with the new-fangled eight-port cylinder head, complete with fuel-injection and forward facing intake trumpets, all somehow fitted under the bonnet panel of the 'works' Mini Cooper S. Originally developed for Group 5 racing, it was finally homologated, and used by late-model 'works' rally cars.

From late 1967, the Mini Cooper S became 'MkII,' complete with this slightly enlarged front grille which, as far as one can see, had no functional use.

1969: A centre-lock Minilite magnesium wheel was evolved, and used on the Tour de France, but not on any other mainstream rally cars.

The majority of 'works' Mini Cooper S-types covered in this book were 1275S types. The author counts no fewer than 48 such cars (identified by registration number) built between 1964 and 1970 inclusive.

According to eminent BMC rally historian Bill Price, the 'works' team actually used only one of the MkIII variety (the final type of production car built in 1970/1971). This was YMO 881H – one of the two cars sent out to Australia in the late summer of 1970, to compete in the Southern Cross Rally, and which apparently was never returned to the UK afterwards.

Mini Cooper 1275GT (used 1970)

Used only for a few months in 1970, as competition cars these machines were effectively re-bodied evolutions of the final type of 1275S, complete with square-nose styling, and therefore they came in for little unique preparation treatment. Effectively these were ultimate-specification 1275S types, but with the new squared-up noses and panelwork. Abingdon, in any case, was suffering from increasingly severe budget constraints, which rather fettered what could be attempted.

British Leyland introduced the long-nose 1275GT in 1969, but it was of little use to the Competitions Department. A handful of competition cars were built in 1970 – including the last cars of all, unused. This particular standard car is using 12in road wheels, which were fitted to all road cars from the mid-1970s.

Abingdon, in fact, used only two such cars, both originally prepared to Group 6 'prototype' specification. They were registered as XJB 308H and SOH 878H. XJB 308H competed in the World Cup (retired with engine problems) and Scottish (second place) rallies of 1970, while SOH 878H was entered in the 84-Hour Marathon de la Route at the Nürburgring in 1970.

In the summer of 1970, two other Clubman/1275GT-type cars, complete with cast-iron eight-port cylinder heads, were also being prepared for use in the Sherry Rally (of Spain), but because the Competitions Department at Abingdon was closed down in the autumn of that year, that entry was withdrawn, and the cars were never used as 'works' entries. These cars, registered YMO 885J and YMO 886J, were not retained after Abingdon's 'Comps' Department closed down, and were sold on as brand-new, un-used, rally cars.

Non-homologated developments

Although what follows could become book length in itself, I ought to explain why some components could not be fitted to a 'works' Mini Cooper, unless it was running outside its normal Group 1 or Group 2 categories. This is how the various Appendix J categories lined up in the mid-1960s:

Group 1: 'Showroom standard' four-seater saloon cars, virtually no modifications allowed. 5000 cars had to be built within 12 months to qualify. Only two extra driving lamps were authorised, and standard 'showroom' seats had to be retained. From January 1966, the 1275S was homologated into Group 1.

    With modifications, a Group 1 car could be upgraded to a Group 2 car – this was done, at Abingdon, on several occasions.

Group 2: Four-seater saloon cars, of which 1000 cars had to be built within a year. Many options were allowed – different gear ratios, different axle ratios and different brake installation kits, for example – but 1000 kits of parts of each had to be made available. Metal could be removed wherever possible (which explains why cylinder head and camshaft profiles could be re-shaped), but not added. Alternative bodyshell material was not allowed.

    By modifying such cars outside the limit of the Group 2 regulations, they could be upgraded to Group 3.

Group 3: Production sports cars, or any car of which 500 had to be built within a year. All Group 2 options could be homologated, along with alternative carburation and exhaust systems to the same Group 2 cylinder head, just so long as 100 had been produced. Light alloy or glass-fibre skin panels of the same shape could be used instead of the standard items; plastic could be used instead of glass windows. Items such as front and rear bumpers could be removed.

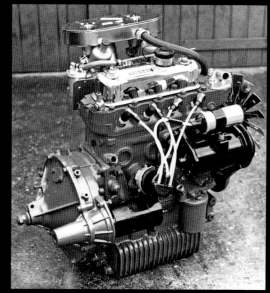

A Group 2-prepared Mini Cooper S engine ready for fitment to a new rally car, showing how the engine sat atop the four-speed transmission. This is the forward-facing aspect of the car.

The same rally-prepared engine viewed from the left side, complete with a 16-bladed cooling fan. This assembly was really a miracle of packaging – and by the mid-1960s well over 100bhp was available from the best 1.3-litre engines.

Group 4 and Group 5: These did not apply to rally cars at this period in history. Even so, Group 5 Mini Cooper S-types were required for British Saloon Car Championship events from 1966 to 1969 inclusive.

Group 6: 'Prototype' cars, for which a minimum production run was not required. Starting from Group 2 or Group 3, almost any or all modifications could be made to those cars, to make them lighter, faster, or more specialised. On Mini Cooper S types, this could mean that non-homologated eight-port cylinder heads (these were later homologated, incidentally), a Weber 40DCOE or fuel-injection induction system, five-speed transmission, or centre-lock/knock-off magnesium road wheels could all be used, as could an extra auxiliary water cooling system.

When running in Group 6, in particular, it was possible to make a Mini Cooper S much lighter, and significantly more powerful than the very best Group 2 car and, because items like the auxiliary cooling system would be fitted, significantly more reliable and long-lived, too.

The above perhaps explains why Group 5 race cars such as those developed by the John Cooper organisation (for use in the British Touring Car Championship), and by the privately financed team of Equipe Arden, were so astonishing fast.

The Cooper/'works' cars eventually used magnesium alloy Minilite wheels with a rim width of no less than eight inches, and fully adjustable front suspension. It was the race cars that first used closing taps in the Hydrolastic lines that linked front and rear suspensions, these eventually being accepted as adjuncts to the shock absorbing system!

It was the engines which received the most attention. All 1275S engines were enlarged to 1293cc (standard bore plus 0.020in re-bore). Although Group 2 engines had to use standard (though polished and internally enlarged) inlet manifolds, on Group 5 and Group 6 cars there was total freedom. First of all, Cooper employed a twin-choke Weber 45DCOE on a special manifold which gave up to 12 extra bhp at close to 6000rpm.

Weslake then evolved a new cross-flow 8-port cylinder head in cast-iron (the inlet ports pointed forwards, and had to be matched to fuel-injection with individual curving inlet trumpets) which featured on engines from 1967. A little later, Downton also devised a dry sump lubrication system which liberated even more power. As Brian Moylan's book from Veloce Publishing, *Anatomy of the Works Mini,* makes clear:

"The car with fuel-injection was now producing 100bhp at the wheels … the best 'wet' sump engine fell short of this, and the best Weber-carbed version gave 88-90 which was about 112bhp at the flywheel. The dry sump engine, although never tested on a dynamometer, was estimated to be giving around 122bhp at the flywheel …"

In some ways, the private-enterprise engine developed by Jim Whitehouse for Equipe Arden was even more remarkable. Whitehouse developed

Here's a rarity – a 1275GT fully modified for motorsport, complete with the eight-port cylinder head, and with four forward-facing Amal carburettors.

his own type of light-alloy eight-port cylinder head, mated it with a 970S engine, and claimed that it was the 115bhp@9000rpm output (allied to Tecalemit fuel-injection and a Colotti five-speed gearbox cluster) which helped Alec Poole to win the 1969 BTCC series by totally dominating his class.

Before the 'works' team efforts finally wound down, the eight-port cylinder heads – the Weslake cast-iron and the Whitehouse/Arden light-alloy – were both homologated.

Was the Mini Cooper unique?

Although there are those who say that any number of businesses could have developed the Mini Cooper into a race and rally-winning machine, I doubt if any operation other than the BMC 'works' team at Abingdon could have turned it into such a formidable little machine so quickly, and kept it at the top for such a lengthy period.

The Mini Cooper pedigree was unique in several ways, but it was the original 850 which took the word 'unique' to its limits. When it was designed, in the late 1950s, other cars had been put on sale with front-wheel-drive, but none had ever packaged a layout in such a successful way. The 850, in other words, was the very first production car to combine a transversely-mounted four-cylinder engine, a transmission system under that engine (rather than behind it, or at one end of it), front-wheel-drive, and rubber-in-compression suspension, all in a miraculously tiny ten-foot-long package.

Other front-wheel-drive cars were, of course, available for rallying in the early 1960s, but were not nearly as competitive as the Minis. Two obvious brands – Saab and DKW – come to mind, but both relied on two-stroke engines, both were considerably bigger and heavier than the Minis, and in neither case was it possible for a private owner to get all the 'works' pieces needed to turn an average road car into something rather special.

Moving on from this, the Mini Cooper was the first British brand to combine an existing marque name with that of a famous race car constructor who had been involved in its development. It was not actually the world's first –

Renault had already got together with Gordini to work the same sort of miracle in France, for instance – but it certainly set a trend in the UK.

The Mini Cooper, however, was definitely the first of a saloon-car breed now known throughout motorsport as the 'homologation special.' This defines a car which was developed with motorsport in mind, one originally intended to be built in small quantities, just enough to keep the FIA inspectors happy, where its ultimate profitability as a production-car programme was not considered vitally important. In cases like that, performance (potential performance in some respects) was always considered more important than refinement, and the potential for power-tuning was also built in.

'Homologation specials' had already been built in other European countries – the Alfa Romeo Giulietta SZ coupé of 1958 being an ideal case in point – though these were sports two-seaters, not four-door saloons. Once the Mini Cooper set the trend, saloons as diverse as the Ford Lotus-Cortina, the Alfa Romeo Giulia TI Super, and the Renault R8 Gordini all joined in.

In parallel with this, there was another aspect of the Mini Cooper/Mini Cooper S which made the car stand out from its rivals – that it was easily possible for a well-to-do private owner to build himself an absolute 'works' replica, as all but a few ultra-secret tweaks were readily available through Abingdon, or through the Special Tuning offshoot. This helped the 'works' operation considerably: on several occasions, when Stuart Turner or Peter Browning needed to make up teams at far-flung events when only an isolated 'works' car was due to be present, they were usually able to draft in well-presented privately owned cars to make up the numbers.

Building and running the 'works' cars

By the time the Mini Cooper was announced in the autumn of 1961, the 'works' motorsport department at Abingdon – often known as 'Comps' – had been up and running for nearly seven years. Although the workshops were contained within a factory block which was part of the ageing complex where hundreds of Austin-Healey and MG sports cars were assembled every week, both functionally and administratively they operated as a separate little empire.

In the Mini Cooper S era, the workforce consisted of a manager (Stuart Turner until 1967, Peter Browning thereafter), his deputy (Bill Price), one or two secretaries, a small group of top mechanics/foremen (Doug Watts, Douggie Hamblin, Tommy Wellman and Den Green being principal characters), along with a group of highly-skilled fitters/mechanics who were expected to tackle anything connected with the preparation of cars. Apart from his normal duties, one of Bill Price's tasks was to look after the homologation, and continual up-dating of paper-work, of the 'works' cars.

Mechanics were not habitually chosen to build cars for a particular driver, but in most cases were merely allocated preparation jobs as these arose. In each and every case, a multi-page Job Sheet would be issued, this sheet becoming gradually more and more complex as the Mini Cooper S' career progressed. A skilled fitter who prepared a Mini Cooper one month, might just have come

from building an Austin-Healey 3000, and might soon be asked to prepare a racing MGB. A given fitter/mechanic would certainly build engines (sourcing all the parts from the stores, including complete cylinder heads and manifolds from Downton Engineering), transmissions, suspensions, and would tackle final assembly. Only the wiring loom, and all electrical installations, would be carried out by specialists from Lucas – in fact, there was so much activity at Abingdon that the Lucas technicians tended to be there, more often than not!

Although Abingdon did much of its own development and improvement, when it came to technical innovation there was constant liaison in several distinctly different directions – with Jack Daniels (Alec Issigonis' chief

Abingdon's workshops were always busy and full of cars – either being prepared for their next event, or refurbished from another outing. Closest to the cameras is one of the 'LBL … D' fleet of 1967, complete with fibreless wheel-arch extensions, and a full Group 2 engine, including 1.5in SU carburettors.

BMC kept the Mini Cooper S at its peak for so long by a lot of attention to fine detail. In this 1968 shot, notice the padded covers over the driving lamps, the Perspex covers over the headlamps, the use of a heated front screen for icy conditions, and the use of mud-flaps ahead of the front wheels to prevent the lamps getting dirty.

mechanical designer at Longbridge, near Birmingham), with Eddie Maher (BMC's chief engine development engineer, based at 'Morris Engines' in Coventry, with Daniel Richmond (who ran Downton Engineering in Wiltshire), and (on racing matters) with John Cooper in south-west London.

In almost every case, the fleet of 'works' rally cars was prepared and maintained at Abingdon. Usually, the process would start with newly-built standard road cars being delivered direct from the Mini assembly lines at Longbridge (Mini Coopers were never built at Cowley, which would have been geographically much more convenient), after which they would be stripped back to the empty painted-bodyshell state, and a long and patient build up to (usually) Group 2 or Group 6 standard begun.

Why did the process not start from a previously sourced

Because 'works' Mini Cooper S cars needed a special wiring loom, Lucas positioned John Smith as its near-resident technician. Tens of hours of work were needed to equip a new rally car in this way.

With all the lights uncovered, and the sun very low over the horizon, this is clearly an early morning shot of Tony Fall's 'works' Mini.

bare shell? As Veloce Publishing author Bryan Moylan has written in *The Anatomy of a Works Mini*:

"Disassembling a standard car and starting from scratch was preferable to trying to order a complete car, with its dozens of brackets, screws, bolts and other items, piecemeal. Stripping it of the major components only took a day to complete, and the conversion to a rally car could begin."

It is worth noting, however, that no 'works' Mini was ever originally intended to have a long life – indeed, in non-romantic terms, they were often treated as consumables. New cars (often for Monte Carlo, and always for a major event) would often suffer a real battering on rough-road events like the Acropolis Rally, or might suffer major damage in an accident (because of the pace at which these cars were driven, this was almost inevitable), and might therefore have to be re-born around a new bodyshell: side-by-side renovations were often seen at Abingdon in those days – and the old shells would either be scrapped, or sold off cheaply, without guarantee, to 'deserving cases.'

In all cases, it was usual for a new car to tackle perhaps two major events, then find itself being used for practice/training for a time, finally being relegated to testing – and eventually to be re-born around a new shell. This explains why a car like GRX 310D tackled the 1966 RAC Rally (November) but did not re-appear until the 1967 French Alpine (September), or why GRX 5D had at least four different bodyshells in a two-year career.

Even so, and although it is always an imperfect way of identifying a separate car, the use of a registration plate (and the appropriate chassis plate) is as good a method as we have, though we must never believe in these without a questioning mind. As previous historians have confirmed, between 1961 and 1970 a considerable number of different cars can be identified. In almost every case, these numbers came from the licensing authorities in Oxford. When a car was re-shelled, the original registration plate would be transferred to the new shell. This explains why, in later years, more than one miraculous restoration by a 'classic' Mini Cooper enthusiast might lay claim to the same Abingdon registration number …

Servicing the hard way – a wheel change is brewing, and in those days there were no high-tech/quick-lift jacks to help the process.

The same team of specialists who developed and prepared the cars usually serviced and supported them in the events themselves, their numbers sometimes being swelled by respected private owners, by specialist fitter/mechanics, or those on the fringes of the team: when major events like Monte Carlo or the French Alpine were in progress, the workshops at Abingdon would be virtually deserted. Service cars – some of them very rare (such as the prototype Vanden Plas Princess R Estate car) – were also used for general transport while the team was back at base. In those days the practice of using vans had not yet become usual, though very occasionally a transporter, which could carry cars to and from circuits, was pressed into service.

Abingdon's team developed several features which were later copied by its rivals. Early in the 1960s, the team

By taking on, and refining, a feature they used with Austin-Healey and MGB race cars, the mechanics sometimes employed quick-lift jacks, which allowed super-rapid wheel changes. The occasional use of centre-lock Minilite road wheels has already been mentioned.

I must also mention the increasingly common practice of gaining easy access to the underside of a 'works' Mini by tipping it over to one side, and using rubber or foam mats on the ground to minimise any scratching or damage which the underside of the car might suffer. Co-driver Mike Wood claims that this stratagem was first employed on John Wadsworth's car in the 1964 Spa-Sofia-Liège, but it became more routine thereafter.

No time, no time – ace mechanic Den Green rushes to complete his work on the 1968 Monte, while driver Rauno Aaltonen waits politely to get on with the job. Their reward, days later, was to take third overall.

built up a mobile petrol tanker, originally for use on the Spa-Sofia-Liège Rally, where petrol supplies in Yugoslavia and Bulgaria were of very doubtful quality, and petrol stations few and far between – this comprising a large rubber bag mounted in a two-wheel trailer which was then towed behind one of the big service cars of the period.

Paddy Hopkirk refuels 33 EJB from a friendly BP tanker in a remote part of France, during the 1964 Monte Carlo rally. Rallying was a much more primitive business in those days. (Reproduced from the BP/Castrol Archive)

The use of a forklift truck to lift cars for underside inspection, immediately after an early special stage on the 1964 RAC Rally, was merely a publicity stunt, and was never intended to be repeated.

Because more and more private owners asked for cars to be prepared to 'works' standard, and the real factory team had no spare time to do this, in the mid-1960s a small, capable, and very successful Special Tuning Operation was set up at Abingdon, managed by Basil Wales, and using its own workshop. At times of real overload (and when a single car was due to be sent out on a less significant international event), a 'works' car would be allocated to Special Tuning, who not only re-prepared it, but supported it on the event itself, often with great success.

Over the years, the 'Comps' Department built up a huge amount of expertise, of records, and of methods, this being something which the dead hand of corporate

There was nothing glamorous about rallying, in winter, in the 1960s – this is one of the 'works' Minis getting new studded tyres at a service point on the Monte Carlo Rally.

politics could not kill. When British Leyland decreed that Abingdon was to close in 1970, a degree of anarchy instantly spread through the ranks where, to their great credit, much of the heritage of this proud department was preserved. As team boss Peter Browning later wrote:

"One policy instruction that epitomised the new management's attitude to Competitions was that all of the department's records, the treasured build sheets for all the cars going back to the 1950s, and the photo library, were to be destroyed. One of my last jobs before I left Abingdon was to ensure that this instruction was ignored, and that this material was saved! ..."

It wasn't only the 'works' cars which became well-known. Dunlop competitions manager David Hiam bought and fitted out this 850, registered it 16 BOJ, and enjoyed some success with it in British events.

Personalities and star drivers

Marcus Chambers

Although Marcus Chambers left BMC just days before the Mini Cooper was launched, he had a pivotal part in planning its arrival. In 1960 and 1961 he co-operated with John Cooper in helping to turn the innocuous little 850cc Mini into a much more promising machine.

Marcus (nicknamed 'Chub' or 'The Poor Man's Neubauer,' because of his bulky build and obvious authority) already had a great background in motorsport before he joined BMC at Abingdon at the end of 1954. Having worked as racing team manager at HRG in 1947 and 1948 (he had driven for the team at Le Mans in 1938 and 1939), he had served with honour in the Royal Navy during the war, and later worked on government schemes in Tanganyika and British Honduras before opening up the new Abingdon Competitions Department under John Thornley's overall control.

Starting from scratch, and after struggling to convert the MG Car Club-based 'works' team that he inherited (the drivers were really from a 'good chaps club') into a quasi-professional organisation, he gradually turned the BMC team into a formidable rallying force. Taking good advice wherever it was offered (and most particularly from John Gott, 'the rallying Policeman,' who was his team captain), he never let work get entirely in the way of good living. Although he gradually built up his on-events service support operation, and went out on as many events as possible, whenever he had to choose between standing outside at a control or service point in the cold and rain, or enjoying a good meal with fine wine, the meal often came first.

It's easy to forget that Marcus had to control a big team on events which were often much more far-flung than in the modern era, and that e-mail, mobile phones, satellite navigation, GPS, fax machines and computers had not been invented. His organisation – and it really was an organisation – coped by planning meticulously before the events, relying on his drivers to make many of their own decisions, and by using the telephone network of whatever country he was in: some of those telecommunications systems were still unreliable, and caused no end of heartache.

Although he was no great shakes as a competition driver, very occasionally Marcus would enter rallies himself, and sometimes he would go out on practice sessions, so he was usually well in touch with the progress of his cars, and of the opposition.

In the seven years that he ran the BMC team (his first autobiography was titled *Seven Year Twitch!*) he nurtured a lot of new driving talent. His biggest 'find,' no question, was the remarkable Pat Moss who, with her good friend and co-driver Ann Wisdom, proved to be an ultra-fast driver – not just a good lady driver, but an ultra-competitive 'bloke' too. Not only that, but when he decided to move on in 1961 (to take up a post in the retail motor trade), he was personally involved in choosing Stuart Turner as his successor.

[Marcus came back to motorsport in 1964, running the Rootes Group's fortunes from 1964 to 1968, which included victory in the London-Sydney Marathon.]

Stuart Turner

Although Turner's best-selling autobiography was titled *Twice Lucky*, few observers thought there was much luck about his glittering career, and the way that it evolved over the years. Not only did he enjoy six remarkably successful years at Abingdon from 1961 to 1967, in later years (from 1969 to 1990), he was one of the top decision-makers in Ford Motorsport, too.

After completing his National Service in the RAF, where he learned enough Russian to be asked to take up a permanent surveillance job in Europe, Turner returned to his native Stone, in Staffordshire, and went on to train, rather un-enthusiastically, as an accountant. At the same time, he took up rallying, always as a co-driver, eventually becoming the most successful in the country.

Having won the BTRDA's National Co-driver Award on three occasions in the 1950s, and become the observant editor of his local motor club magazine (where he was famous for his mordant humour), he branched out even further by tackling European events. Not only did he become instantly famous in November 1960 by navigating the giant Swede Erik Carlsson to victory in the British RAC International Rally, but also the first-ever Rallies Editor ('Verglas') of *Motoring News*.

He always insisted that he was surprised to be offered the job of BMC Competitions Manager in 1961, but took to it with alacrity, and great skill. Although he admitted that he could not have arrived at a more favourable time (the Mini Cooper was new, and the Healey 3000 still approaching maturity), he introduced an atmosphere of ruthless purpose to a still improving team.

Within a year, some of the Old Guard of drivers and co-drivers had been eased out, though Turner made sure that Pat Moss remained. Other new arrivals were Timo Makinen and Rauno Aaltonen (the original 'Flying Finns'), Paddy Hopkirk and, eventually, deep-thinking co-drivers such as Tony Ambrose, Paul Easter and Henry Liddon. However, not even Turner could persuade Pat Moss to remain at Abingdon throughout her career, for she accepted a big financial offer from Ford at the end of 1962.

Team manager Stuart Turner (wearing glasses) conferring with Timo Makinen in Monte Carlo in 1967, when a crucially important choice of tyres had to be made.

Not only that, but it was under Turner's control that the team got down to some more serious technical development, to work with Dunlop, to refine its reconnaissance and pace-noting expertise, to tighten up its service procedures, and to be even more aggressive with new homologation, the way a professional team should be run.

By pushing every aspect of this job to the limits – not least by a careful study of homologation and event regulations – Stuart was able to optimise the performance of an already very capable team. As an experienced competitor and strategist, and not merely a good manager, of course

he had the confidence of his drivers, who performed better than they might have done for anyone else.

Everyone was surprised when Turner abruptly decided to leave BMC at the beginning of 1967, especially after telling everyone that he thought he no longer wanted to climb mountains, stand at the side of the road getting soaked, or have to answer to his bosses for the vagaries of event organisers.

This was the moment when he handed over to Peter Browning, in as smooth a transition as could be wished, and Peter ran the Mini Cooper S team for the next four years. Even so, after spending just two years with the oil company Castrol (latterly as publicity manager), Stuart had yet another change of mind, seduced back into the sport by Ford-UK, and spent the next two decades running motorsport and public affairs for the company.

Peter Browning

How could it be that London-born Browning started life building church organs, and achieved fame as BMC's third Competitions Manager, when the Mini Cooper S was at the height of its career? As ever, 'happenstance' had much to do with this – but in the 1960s Peter's growing reputation as a time-keeper, race-team manager and enthusiastic motor sport administrator all helped.

After starting work at Abingdon in 1958, to found and build up an Austin-Healey Club, Peter went on to become a race time-keeper for Geoff Healey, graduated to running the MGB race efforts at Le Mans and elsewhere, and was an obvious candidate to succeed Stuart Turner in 1967. Pitched into the Manager's chair with only weeks to plan, he soon became much respected around the world of rallying (about which, he claims, had had very little experience at first), and guided the Mini Cooper S to full maturity, with five European Championship wins in 1967 alone.

From 1968, British Leyland took over management control from BMC, Mini Cooper S fortunes slumped as other priorities were imposed on the famous Abingdon department, and Peter found motorsport increasingly frustrating. Real progress and great success with cars as varied as BMC 1800s and Triumph 2.5PIs was not thought good enough by the philistines at British Leyland's head office, the operation was closed down in 1970, and Peter walked away from the wreckage.

Occasionally, just occasionally, rival team managers talked to each other. Stuart Turner (left) of BMC discussing some point on the French Alpine Rally of 1964 with Alan Platt of Ford.

In later years he not only became Executive Director at the British Racing and Sports Car Club (BRSCC), but ran a thriving media photo service for Marlboro, before being attracted back to run the motorsport side of the vast MG Car Club.

Bill Price

Every business needs its unsung heroes, to allow them to survive without drama. Such characters rarely reach the pinnacle of the concern or see much limelight, but without them things simply would not work as smoothly as they should. At Abingdon, from 1960 to 1970, and when both the Healey and the Mini Coopers were at their peak, Bill Price was that man, with the bulging files, the background information, and the mass of material held from previous events to allow all planning for the future to be seamless.

When the department re-opened in 1974 after its period of suspended animation, he speedily came back from a deadly routine job in the retail motor trade, and stayed with what was now British Leyland until the last of the Triumph TR7 V8 rally cars was retired after the end of the 1980 season.

It was only after Bill produced his monumental book *BMC/BL Competitions Department* (Veloce) in the 1990s that many people realised just what careful records he had been storing away for so many years. As one colleague commented at the time: "We thought he just didn't want to share a pint with us in the evenings – it now seems that he was always upstairs in his room, updating his diary …"

Having completed his trade apprenticeship at Morris Commercial, and then his National Service, Bill joined the Competitions Department at Abingdon as a lowly office assistant. Before long he was seen to be much more capable than that, taking over new homologation duties, much of the workshop organisation, and acting as Marcus Chambers,' then Stuart Turner's, stand-in team manager on many events.

Bill was one of those invaluable team players who 'oil the wheels' and fill in the gaps. It was Bill who would fly out to the start of events with urgently needed spares, or fly off to the back of beyond to retrieve broken or crashed rally cars, and square the authorities or BMC dealers who had had to be ignored in the rush of events. He also knew more about the shopfloor staff than his bosses ever did, and was an invaluable link between them and management hierarchy.

Meticulous as a planner, forgetting little about past events and experiences, and always ready to sort out last-minute crises, he effectively became Deputy Competitions Manager well before the title was officially conferred on him. Before, and increasingly after, he retired, he built up more 'I was there' knowledge of the famous BMC 'works' team than any other surviving team member, and has confirmed much of the detail information in this book.

Pat Moss

Everyone loved Pat Moss. I have never found anyone with a word to say against her. Although she arrived in rallying in 1955 with the damning designation 'Stirling's little sister' hanging around her neck, within a couple of years she had shown just how fast, tough and capable she was going to be as a rally driver. Within five years of joining the BMC team, she had not only become a credible lady rally driver, but had actually won the toughest of all rallies, outright, in an Austin-Healey 3000 – the Liège-Sofia-Liège.

A relatively latecomer to rallying (she had spent her earlier years competing in horse jumping events, at which she was also adept), she eventually started at BMC by driving an uncompetitive MG TF on the 1955 RAC Rally, though her next drive was delayed until the Monte Carlo of 1956. After graduating to Morris Minor 1000s and MG MGAs, she got her first chance to wrestle with the Big Healey (a 100-Six) on the French Alpine of 1958, and would drive one of the first 'works' Mini Coopers in 1962.

By that time there was no doubt that this slight, devastatingly pretty, and (outwardly only) insecure young lady had become an established member of the team. Although she seemed scatterbrained to a fault (many was the time when she left her handbag behind at an hotel, restaurant, or rally service point!), and liked to trade on the 'wide-eyed innocent' reputation which developed over time, she was nevertheless ferociously competitive, with great endurance and a real will to win.

Always a heavy smoker – it took its toll in later years – and seemingly hyperactive (she disliked having nothing to do, and would always be on the lookout for a diversion …) she liked to be busy-busy, and was apparently interested in anything which life had to offer. Her rallying partnership with Ann Wisdom (the daughter of Fleet Street's motoring doyen, Tommy Wisdom) worked very well, the two not only being a professional success, but great friends, too.

Once she came to terms with the Big Healey (she always said it frightened her, but then so did Paddy Hopkirk – and they both won events in the cars …) she was often as fast as all but the two Flying Finns, and was already being measured, and compared, on a daily basis, by all her peers. Though broad-shouldered, with enough body strength to cope with these big cars, Pat was strictly the sort of active, sport-loving lady who disarmed most men with her charm – yet she could also become depressed if the cars were not always in good health. Converting to Mini Coopers was surprisingly straightforward, she became competitive at once, and really flew the Mini Cooper flag in the only season (1962) in which she drove such cars.

Each of her cars got nicknames (her Liège-winning Healey, URX 727, was soon known as 'Uurrxx,' her long-lived Morris 1000 was 'Granny,' while a singularly unlucky Healey 3000 was always known as 'The Thing'), and of course she had her own foibles about equipment. Like big brother Stirling, she liked her car registration numbers, and competition numbers, to have a '7' in them – but she disliked the number '13.'

Once the Mini Cooper arrived, she was even more successful in that little car, and the workshop staff at Abingdon were almost ready to walk through fire to build her a good example of any rally car.

Having met the mountainous Swedish rally driver Erik Carlsson, the two rapidly became an item, and Pat eventually married him in 1962. For 1963, both were courted by Ford (which offered big financial incentives, that BMC could not match): Pat took up that offer, though Erik did not. Later, Pat moved on to drive, with Erik, at Saab and, later, Lancia, but she was never seen as a total icon for those teams, not in the same way that she had always been at BMC.

When she died in 2008, there was general sadness in motorsport, for lady drivers of her calibre were, and are, very thin on the ground.

Paddy Hopkirk

Behind the Irish blarney, and the readiness to share a quip, and to give quotable quotes to any motoring writer, Paddy Hopkirk's genial facade hid a rally driver with steely determination, yet someone who never quite achieved as much as he thought he deserved. Amazingly enough, his most prestigious of several victories – in the 1964 Monte in a Mini Cooper 1071S – was achieved without making any fastest stage times in the event, and in three years he recorded only one outright victory in a Big Healey (Austrian Alpine 1964). Even so, he was always competitive – sometimes aggressively so – in Minis. For all that, he became Fleet Street's favourite rallying personality, and kept that fame for more than thirty years after he retired.

Having begun his rallying career as a driving test specialist in Northern Ireland, Paddy then started his 'works' career with Standard-Triumph in 1956. After falling out with Triumph team manager Ken Richardson in 1958 (as the rallying 'circus' knew well, that was not difficult), he left the team to join the Rootes Group team of Sunbeam Alpines and Rapiers. It was only in 1962, and with the Rapiers apparently at their peak, that he approached Stuart Turner at BMC, proposing himself to join the team and (in his own words) 'to get his hands on the Healey 3000.' In a letter to Turner at this time he wrote that: "I want to drive cars which are capable of winning rallies outright – even if I'm not!"

Even though he soon came to terms with the high performance, but rather brutal character of that car – he took second place, overall, in the 1962 RAC behind Erik Carlsson's all-conquering Saab 96, and finished sixth in the 1963 RAC Rally – Paddy always admitted that he never quite mastered and fourth in the London-Mexico World Cup Rally (in a big Triumph 2.5PI saloon).

In a Mini Cooper S, though, Paddy became a master. His 1964 Monte victory quite overshadowed equally meritorious runs, including that phenomenal Tour de France performance of 1963, two Circuit of Ireland successes, and both the Acropolis and French Alpine victories in 1967.

In his very successful BMC/British Leyland years, which continued until the entire department closed down in 1970, Paddy was a good and supportive 'team player' to the 'Flying Finns' which, to those who had known him in his Triumph and Rootes Group days, came as a real surprise. The big difference, though, was that there was a huge and constantly growing sense of team spirit at Abingdon, which had never existed in other teams. Not only that, but Paddy studiously developed his good relations with the press, and became a very valuable 'front man' for the rally team.

Rauno Aaltonen

One of the original 'Flying Finns' in the 'works' rally team of the 1960s, Rauno became the single most successful Mini rally driver at BMC, and also the man who delivered the most prestigious Healey victory of all time – in the 1964 Spa-Sofia-Liège Marathon Rally. As an analytical and a compulsive re-designer of all his rally cars, Rauno did as much as anyone to keep the Mini Cooper S and the Healey 3000 improving in the 1960s.

First as a private owner in Finland, then in vast 'works' Mercedes-Benz saloons, he caught team boss Stuart Turner's eye in those cars on the 1961 Polish and RAC rallies, and was rapidly signed up for 1962. After starting in a (privately supported) Cooper in the 1962 Monte (where he was nearly killed in a fiery crash which trapped him in an upside-down wreck), he rapidly became a fully-fledged BMC 'works' team member in mid-1962, and was the original 'Flying Finn.'

Even during the 1964 Monte, which he won, Paddy still had time to talk to fellow Irishman Ernest MacMillan at a control point on the way to the principality. (Reproduced from the BP/Castrol Archive)

the Healey, and that he eventually became much more relaxed when driving the 'works' Mini Cooper S instead.

Even so, he went on to win the 1964 Austrian Alpine Rally (in ARX 91B, the second of the newly-prepared wind-up window Austin-Healey BJ8s), and was impressive in Healeys on the race track. In some cases, however, Paddy was an unlucky 'nearly man' – as shown by his second place (in a BMC 1800) in the London-Sydney Marathon of 1968,

What every well-dressed rally driver was wearing in 1966/1967 – this was Rauno Aaltonen, complete with Dunlop racing overalls, watching his 1275S being serviced.

Rauno Aaltonen (right) and Tony Ambrose won the European Rally Championship for BMC, driving Mini Cooper S types, in 1965. (Reproduced from the BP/Castrol Archive)

Some of his most noteworthy victories were in Mini Cooper S-types – he notched up his first outright win in the French Alpine Rally of 1963 – for Rauno won no fewer than nine Internationals in Minis, including five in 1965 alone, when he became European Rally Champion. Among his famous victories were the 1965 RAC Rally and the 1967 Monte.

Rauno was always super-smooth as a driver, and only rarely a crasher. He was always the team's great thinker, the one with the most good ideas, and with the tendency to sketch up those ideas on the back of envelopes, service schedules, and even on restaurant tablecloths. Some found his compulsion to fiddle with specifications rather irritating, but others found his mild, good mannered, character very appealing. Even so, when super-fast times were needed, no-one delivered more consistently than Rauno.

Even when the Healey's front-line life as a rally car ended, Rauno was still reaching his personal peak, and he

No other rally car ever handled as well as the 'works' Mini, not even approaching its nimble standards. Rauno Aaltonen, seen on a tarmac hairpin of the Monte Carlo rally, was one of the world's very best Mini drivers.

went on to achieve even greater things for BMC driving Mini Cooper Ss. In 1968, after the formation of British Leyland, Rauno didn't really leave the team, rather the team left him. When Lord Stokes demanded big changes at Abingdon, Rauno's (and Timo Makinen's) contract was quite unforgiveably torn up at the end of that season. Having dabbled with Lancia and, in later years, with Nissan, Rauno became a much-sought-after ambassador for European manufacturers like BMW. To his great sorrow he never won the Safari, though he finished second on four occasions.

Unlike other stars of the 1960s, Rauno rarely got involved in the growing and glamorous world of Historic rallying, preferring to make his living as a teacher, and representative of various manufacturers. With BMW, he once demonstrated the crash test capability of a restraint system by taking the place of the 'dummy:' Rauno, naturally, had done all his research in advance, and knew it was safe.

Timo Makinen

From the time he first saw him, to this day, when questioned about his illustrious past, BMC rally team boss Stuart Turner has no doubts, that Timo (the second of the 'Flying Finns') was the fastest rally driver in the world. For more than a decade – 1962 until the mid-1970s – Timo probably started

Throughout the 'works' Mini period which covered the 1960s, Timo Makinen was undoubtedly the fastest, if not always the luckiest, of the team's drivers. Along with his co-driver, Paul Easter, he always excited the crowd. ORX 77F was brand-new for the 1968 Monte. This was not one of Abingdon's 'lucky' cars.

every rally as the favourite, and led most of them. Although he rarely crashed, he was hard on his cars, expecting his team to build machinery which would withstand his methods.

Originally something of a wild-man in his native Finland (among his exploits was racing a Jaguar D-type on ice, on spiked tyres!), Timo got a trial in the BMC 'works' team after the Finnish importer called Stuart Turner to plead his case. Within a year he had mastered Mini Coopers and Austin-Healey 3000s, and no-one else could match him.

Like other BMC team members of the day, Timo won many major Internationals in Mini Cooper Ss, while in a later sporting life he also won three RAC Rallies in Ford Escorts. He seemed to lead almost every rally he ever started, though

his machinery often let him down. Observers reckon that his 1965 Monte victory (in a Mini Cooper S) was the best rally drive of all time, but others remember that 1965 RAC Rally in a Healey 3000, where he was demonstrably the fastest of all on snow, ice, deep mud, and sometimes hard gravel. He was only robbed of victory by Rauno Aaltonen's Mini Cooper S, which could get more grip, more often.

In a word, as a rally driver Timo was spectacular and, let us be honest, almost impossible to control by his co-drivers. When the situation demanded it (and at other times, too, when he felt like it), Timo was a more flamboyant driver than any of his team mates, more sideways, more energetic, and behind the wheel was demonstrably putting

Timo Makinen (left) and Henry Liddon were both important members of the BMC rally team in the 1960s.

more effort into his driving than they were. A co-driver had to be brave to control such a massive personality, and it was the mild-mannered Paul Easter who managed this best of all.

When Timo and his car were on song, no-one – not even Rauno Aaltonen, certainly not Paddy Hopkirk – could match his pace in similar machines. To see Timo in full flow – particularly from the terrifying vantage point of the passenger seat – was an awe-inspiring experience. Certainly he drove his cars harder than anyone else of the period, expecting them to put up with his brutal methods, and to withstand assault from the rough special stage tracks.

As with Rauno Aaltonen, Timo left the BMC team in 1968 after Lord Stokes culled the department. Since the Mini Cooper S was already over its peak by that time, he was, in any case, falling out with the team, and despised the BMC 1800 'Landcrabs' which were replacing the Minis.

Later, ex-BMC team boss Stuart Turner persuaded him to join the Ford team in 1970, and he then enjoyed seven seasons at Boreham. Three RAC Rally wins in Escorts were a highlight of this time, but there were other individual successes too. Ford management did not always enjoy his meddling with specifications, though, and he was released at the end of 1976.

Tony Fall

Yorkshire-born Tony was the last, the youngest, and the most extrovert of what became known as BMC's 'Famous Five' – the others, of course, being Rauno Aaltonen, Paddy Hopkirk, Timo Makinen and Pat Moss – all of whom mastered the Mini Cooper S, and recorded many a famous victory in the cars.

Coming on to the rally scene in 1965, when he forced his way into the team by sheer talent and British north-country brashness, he had started in club events with cars from his employer's BMC car dealership. Hired at BMC by Stuart Turner as the 'apprentice,' he rapidly learned his trade, and started winning at international level within months. In the next two seasons he won four major events – a good strike rate by any standards – and endeared himself to the team with his extrovert, ready-to-learn, enthusiastic manner.

Like Paddy Hopkirk, Tony Fall was a 'good interview,' so before, during or after events the media were always happy to listen to his views, especially in the bar, with a beer in front of him. He was young enough and fit enough to undertake the weeks of practice that top-line rallying seemed to need in those days. As to his driving methods – not as rough as Timo, and not as silky-smooth as Rauno – he

was hard on his cars, and was always likely to go towards the very edge of an accident when pressed. Although this did not endear him to BMC's accountants, it always made him 'good copy' for the specialist magazines.

In some ways Tony was unlucky, for – almost by definition – he was fourth in the BMC 'pecking order' from 1966 to 1968, behind established superstars. In any other team, he would have shone like a true lead driver, and become as legendary as – say – Paddy Hopkirk had already become.

After 1968, Tony had an eventful further career – as driver, team manager and business man. In the early 1970s he drove for Ford-UK, BMW, Nissan, VW and Lancia. He then became competitions manager of Opel in Germany, and after being unjustly accused of laundering sponsorship moneys at Opel, returned to the UK, where he eventually took control of the Safety Devices roll cage concern. In recent years, he became an enthusiastic competitor in classic rallies, then tragically died (of a heart attack) at the end of 2007.

Tony Fall soon settled in alongside Paddy Hopkirk and the Flying Finns, and by the time the Mini reached its peak, was as fast as any of them.

Tony Fall (left) and Mike Wood came together at BMC, in Minis, in the mid-1960s, and notched up many victories for the team. The backdrop is Monte Carlo in 1966.

Competition story

The 'works' Mini Cooper's career

Once the first Mini Cooper had been launched, the 'works' Competitions Department lost no time in getting it homologated, and ready for action, but of course they had to wait until the requisite number of production cars had been built. First, however, the new Competition Manager, Stuart Turner, had to convince himself that his future strategy was sound – namely that he would concentrate on the use of Mini Coopers, Austin-Healey 3000s, and that occasionally he would add an MG to the mix when the regulations favoured its use.

This explains, no doubt, why he entered MG Midgets and Healey 3000s for the 1961 RAC Rally, no fewer than seven different BMC models for the 1962 Monte Carlo Rally (two being publicity/'media' entries), and three MGAs for the 1962 Sebring 12-Hour race. Shortly, however, he and his team were convinced that the Mini Cooper had a long and potentially exciting rally career ahead of it. FIA Homologation was achieved in January 1962, which cleared the way.

Although preparation of two 'works' Mini Coopers began before the end of 1961, these machines – one being 737 ABL, for Pat Moss to drive, the other being registered in the West Country (11 NYB) for Geoff Mabbs – were not intended to compete until 1962, when the Monte Carlo Rally would be an obvious place to start. Homologation was not achieved, incidentally, until 16 January 1962, mere days before the Monte Carlo Rally was due to start.

1962

As mentioned, BMC supported no fewer than eight different cars for the Monte Carlo Rally, one of which was an 850 Mini (for the Rev. Rupert Jones) and two others being the brand-new Mini Coopers (with 997cc engines, the only version available at this stage) for Pat Moss, and Geoff Mabbs/Rauno Aaltonen. Stuart Turner had signed up Rauno as the very first of his 'Flying Finns,' and wisely decided

Not a pretty sight – but fortunately no-one was hurt. Rauno Aaltonen, on his first rally in a Mini Cooper, crashed this car on the descent of the Col du Turini in the 1962 Monte, when it caught fire and burnt out. The cause, it was thought, was a battery cable that had shorted-out against the fuel tank.

to team him with Geoff Mabbs, who had recently won the Tulip Rally outright in a Triumph Herald Coupé.

This was not a good start for the cars. Pat Moss, still new to the model (she had only started one rally in an 850, and that had retired with engine trouble), took time to get used to the handling, and the car suffered from a broken throttle cable at one point. Although down at seventh in her capacity class, at least she won the Ladies' Prize, which was mildly encouraging. She came to love this car – 737 ABL – which no-one else was allowed to drive throughout the year – and in the end it would deliver two outright victories!

The other entry almost ended in tragedy. With Rauno Aaltonen driving all the special stages, the other car (11 NYB) had been positively scurrying along but, on the descent of the Col de Turini, Rauno crashed the car – it turned over on a narrow stretch, and caught fire due to body damage resulting in an electrical short across the battery terminals in the boot.

As historian Peter Browning later wrote: "Trapped by partly melted seat belts, Rauno resigned himself to death and described the experience as 'very peaceful, but warm.'"

Co-driver Geoff Mabbs, however, had more forceful ideas and dragged a comatose Rauno out of the blazing wreckage. Happily, there were no serious personal injuries. The car was a total write-off, but under the circumstances no-one cared about that.

The redoubtable Ms Moss then turned up on the Tulip Rally in May, where 'Able' (Pat always nicknamed her cars) was in sparkling form – it was, incidentally, still the only 'works' Mini Cooper to have been completed. Because the Tulip ran according to a rather difficult-to-understand handicap system – a car needed to be outstandingly faster on the stages than any other in its capacity class – Pat found the speed tests much to her liking. Although 'Able' was still much slower than the 'works' Austin-Healey 3000s which also started, it was the best class car, and, to everyone's delight, ran out as overall winner of the Dutch event.

Pat's co-driver, Ann Wisdom, was doubly delighted – not only because of the outright victory, which followed on the success they had had on the Liège-Rome-Liège marathon in a Big Healey in 1960, but because she had

850 Minis in rallying

Although 'works' Mini 850s were used for two full seasons, their activities could be described as 'brave' rather than successful. Frankly, they were not fast enough, or powerful enough, to do more than fight for lowly class wins – which, of course, explains why the Mini Cooper was developed in the first place.

This programme can really be summarised by these bald statistics. Between September 1959 and May 1962, nine different 'works' 850s started 16 events, winning their capacity class just three times. In all this time, the most meritorious performance was set by David Seigle-Morris in the 1960 RAC Rally, where he won his class and finished sixth overall.

In the early days, development problems were serious – but would all benefit the Mini Cooper programme in the end. First there were slipping clutches (oil leaked on to them from the engine), then steel wheels suffering from early fatigue failures (which caused them to fall off the car!), shock absorbers and front suspension ball joint breakages, and finally transmission problems. When one considers that this was probably the slowest rally car which Abingdon had prepared for some years, this was not all encouraging.

Although these cars were demonstrably too slow – they could not match the performance of the two-stroke Saab 96s, and DKW Juniors – they were, at least, gradually coming to terms with the demands of rallying. In a way this meant that preparation of the first 'works' Mini Coopers would be more straightforward.

recently discovered, to her joy, that she was pregnant (her husband, Peter Riley, was also a member of the BMC team). So, having won the Tulip Rally with two-and-a-half people in the car (in later life Tim Riley, the still-to-be-born baby, had to put up with some ribbing), this combination had to be broken up, on a very high note.

Pat Moss then went off to drive Big Healeys on the French Alpine, so 737 ABL was put into a corner, and the second-ever 'works' 997cc car, 407 ARX, was made ready for Rauno Aaltonen to drive in the French Alpine, and later in the Finnish 1000 Lakes. It was not a good return to Mini Coopers for the Flying Finn, as on the Alpine the new car overheated badly in the mountains of southern France, and suffered severe transmission problems, finally being obliged to retire. The same car retired with mechanical failure on the 'Finnish GP' – which became officially known as the Rally of 1000 Lakes!

In the meantime Bengt Soderstrom (a large man in a tiny car!) had used a BMC-Sweden-prepared 997cc car to win the Swedish Rally to the Midnight Sun, favoured by a class improvement system of marking special stage times, for he was not nearly as fast as Bengtsson's Porsche 356 90, or Erik Carlsson's Saab 96. Still, a win is a win, and since BMC-Sweden's Mini Coopers also won the Manufacturers' Team Prize, there was much celebration back at Abingdon.

This was the point at which Pat Moss and the amazingly small 737 ABL ('Able') came back into the picture. Happily for her, she got on well with her newly appointed co-driver, Pauline Mayman. This was another of those events run on a handicap basis, so although the gallant little Mini Cooper was not the fastest car on the speed hill climbs and other tests, it was quite outstanding in its class. Pat, who never put a foot wrong in this car, and who came to love it, therefore drove it into fourth overall on 'scratch' times, behind a powerful team of Mercedes-Benz saloons, but revelled in the sometimes wet conditions, and won on handicap.

One month later, on the Geneva Rally (which used many familiar speed tests and mountain roads in French Alpine territory) it was almost, but not quite, the same story.

On the road, the fastest cars of all were Hans Walter's Porsche 356 Carrera and Jean-Jacque Thuner's 'works' Triumph TR4, though after all the handicapping and class improvement calculations had been made, Pat and the Mini Cooper finished up third overall, behind Walter and Erik Carlsson's Saab 96.

Then came the British RAC Rally, where team boss Stuart emptied the budget coffers at Abingdon, entering no fewer than eight cars – four Austin-Healey 3000s, an MG1100 and three Mini Coopers. Because Pat Moss was in a Big Healey (she would take third place overall), the Mini Coopers were driven by Rauno Aaltonen (in a modified Group 3 car), Logan Morrison, and an unknown (to the Brits) Finn called Timo Makinen.

As Stuart Turner later admitted: "I knew nothing about Timo Makinen until the autumn of 1962, when Raoul Falin, who was the Morris dealer in Helsinki, came to Abingdon and said: 'I've got this young Finnish driver, Timo Makinen, you won't know him, but I've sometimes lent a car to him for Finnish rallies. He's quick – I think you might be impressed – and it really would help me in Finland if you could find a car for him to drive in the RAC Rally …' ..."

Even though the 1962 RAC – with big road mileage and many Forestry Commission special stages – was once again dominated by Erik Carlsson's front-wheel-drive Saab 96, and the always great 'works' Austin-Healey 3000s, the Mini Coopers (two of them, 977ARX and 477 BBL being brand-new) were impressive and, thank goodness, reliable.

Although it was always clear that none of the Mini pilots could keep up with the Saab, and that the Big Healeys (second and third overall in the end) were much quicker, their general pace and sure-footed handling in the forests was clear. In the early stages, BMC-Sweden Minis driven by Tom Trana and Bengt Soderstrom led all the British 'works' cars (which, at last, allowed BMC PR men to point out that it was the cars, not the special 'you can't buy them over the counter' pieces which were important) and were actually in second and third positions overall, but that was about to change.

On the second part of the rally, from Blackpool to Bournemouth, both the BMC-Sweden cars retired with mechanical breakdowns, the top order of Saab-Healey 3000-Healey 3000 was confirmed, and the only other car to beat Rauno Aaltonen's 'works' Mini Cooper was 'Tiny' Lewis's 'works' Sunbeam Rapier. In the end, the Minis finished fifth (Aaltonen), seventh (Timo) and thirteenth (Logan Morrison). Not only that, but the trio won the Manufacturers' Team Prize, and there were two class victories to celebrate as well. This was a good, if not sensational, way to end the Mini Cooper's first season.

In summary, 'works' Minis had entered seven major rallies, Pat Moss had won two of them outright, all achieved with a fleet of just four cars. Other cars, notably from BMC-Sweden, had shown that the pedigree was widespread.

If there was a downer at the end of the season, it was that Pat Moss accepted a very big financial offer from Ford, to jump ship, and to drive new-model Cortinas in 1963. Although she had won two events for BMC in Mini Coopers, she would never have the chance to see just how good the Mini Cooper S could be ...

1963

Although the new season started well enough, with high placings in the Monte Carlo and Tulip rallies, there was an air of suppressed excitement at Abingdon (and, incidentally, in the John Cooper Racing Team). Although the public knew nothing about this, the teams knew full well that the first of the Mini Cooper S-types – the 1071S – was due to be launched in April, and Bill Price (charged with getting the new car homologated just as soon as possible) was hoping that he would have all the necessary papers approved by May 1963. In this, as we know, he succeeded, and the important up-grade, from using 997cc Mini Coopers to 1071S-types, began at once.

In the meantime, BMC entered no fewer than eight 'works' cars for the Monte Carlo Rally, four of them being the existing fleet of four 997cc-engined cars, all of them refurbished since the end of the 1962 season. The driving team was now looking formidable, for although new recruit Timo Makinen was driving an Austin-Healey 3000, Rauno Aaltonen, Paddy Hopkirk, Logan Morrison and Pauline Mayman were using the Minis.

This particular Monte will always be remembered for the blizzard-conditions which decimated the field though, to their great credit, each of the Mini Coopers struggled through to the finish: only 102 of the 296 starters made it to the Mediterranean. For the media, the big story was the original onslaught from Ford-USA, where Bo Ljungfeldt's Falcon set a string of fastest times (but lost time on the road), but it was other front-wheel-drive cars, led by Erik Carlsson's formidable Saab 96, which set all the standards.

Special stage conditions – fresh snow, almost complete coverage throughout – were good, if not ideal, for the Minis, so the cars were fast, if not quite fast enough to beat the Saab and Paul Toivonen's big Citroën ID19. Rauno Aaltonen took third overall in 977 ARX, Paddy Hopkirk (407 ARX) was sixth behind two more 'works' Citroëns, and, because it had been entered in Group 3 form, Logan Morrison's 477 BBL won its 1-litre GT class too.

Because of the 'class improvement' handicap which still prevailed on the Tulip Rally, BMC then hedged its bets by entering two Austin-Healeys and two Mini Coopers. This time around, Paddy Hopkirk was allocated a brand-new 997cc car (17 CRX), while Pauline Mayman, once again, drove 'Able,' the original Mini Cooper, which was always piloted by a lady driver during its two years at Abingdon. This was another good, if not quite triumphant, outing for the little front-wheel-drive cars, for Paddy Hopkirk took second place overall (though Pauline Mayman struggled to set similarly high standards).

If Pat Moss had not won the 1962 event in 'Able,' everyone would no doubt have been amazed by Paddy's second place – though the class improvement system saw an outstandingly-driven Ford Falcon Sprint (Henri Greder at the wheel) take outright honours: Paddy, in fact, was seventh fastest on scratch times. Incidentally, private owner Julien Vernaeve's fine Mini Cooper drove into third place in the GT category, something which is often missed by the historians.

After Pauline Mayman had then not only won the Ladies Prize, but also her class in the German Trifels (using 'Able' as usual), it was time for a concerted team effort in the French Alpine Rally – there being four 'works' Austin-Healey 3000s and four Minis. Because 1071S homologation had duly been achieved in May 1963, one brand-new car (277 EBL) was made ready for Rauno Aaltonen to drive. Three other 997cc-engined cars were entered – 18 CRX (the very last such 'works' 997 to be prepared) for Pauline Mayman, 977 ARX for John Sprinzel, and 17 CRX was used by USA motoring writer Denise McCluggage.

This particular high summer event is remembered for the wonderful weather in the South of France, for the high rate of attrition in the entry, and the way that mechanical misfortune eliminated six cars. All four Big Healeys retired (two of them because of accidents), John Sprinzel's Mini crashed after the steering broke, and Denise McCluggage's car broke a transmission drive shaft coupling. On the other hand, the really good news was that Pauline Mayman finished sixth and won her class, while Rauno Aaltonen took the still-new/still-under-developed 1071S to outright victory in the Touring Category. It was an outstanding performance, marred only by persistent engine overheating, which the mechanics kept in check by insisting that the car's heater was run full blast throughout (in France, in June – Oh boy!) …

Then, three months later, came the victory which really set the Mini Cooper S on its way to worldwide fame. Because BMC was still taking its time to build up a fleet of 1071S-types, only one such car was entered for the nine-day, 3600 mile (5796km) Tour de France, accompanied by three 997cc Mini Coopers. Paddy Hopkirk's 1071S was 33 EJB, the car which would later become legendary for its 1964 Monte success, and one of the 997cc cars was Rauno Aaltonen's ex-1071S from the French Alpine! Confusing – but demonstrating just how similar the two existing types really were …

This was the event that really made the Mini Cooper S's reputation, for not only was Hopkirk's car consistently very fast, it was reliable, too. In an event which meandered all round France, Belgium and Germany, taking in one-hour or two-hour races at the Nürburgring, Spa, Rheims, Rouen, Le Mans, Pau, Albi and Clermont Ferrand (a total of 12 racing hours), it also encompassed many famous hill climb tests including Mont Ventoux, the Col de Rousset and Chamrousse. This high profile French event was split into Touring and Grand Touring categories (the Minis being Touring, of course), so much of the media glamour focussed on the GT category, where fleets of Ferrari 250GTOs fought it out among themselves. Just as in the British Saloon Car series, the Mini Coopers, however, had to fight against Ford Galaxies, Jaguar MkIIs, Sunbeam Rapiers, Alfa Romeos and the like.

Although two of the 997cc cars – driven by Timo Makinen and Pauline Mayman – retired with mechanical problems, Paddy's brand-new 1071S kept going at remarkable speed, jousting for the Touring Car lead on the twisty circuits. In the end, the Galaxies wilted and the well proven Jaguars prevailed, yet Paddy took a rousing third place overall in Touring and won the prestigious handicap, plus his capacity class, in great style. The French BMC distributor, it is said, was overwhelmed with orders for the new car …

After this the 'works' team needed, and took, an eight-week rest from competition, for the final entry of the season was the RAC Rally, held in November. Once again Stuart Turner split his team's resources, entering three Austin-Healey 3000s and three Mini Coopers. This time there were to be two 1071Ss – a brand-new car (8 EMO) for Paddy Hopkirk, and 277 EBL (re-re-engined – it started life as a 1071S, but had competed in the Tour de France in 997cc engine form!) for Pauline Mayman, while Logan Morrison drove 407 ARX, which was getting somewhat long in the tooth, but still well worth entering in the Group 3 category.

In what was to be a typical RAC – a week-long event starting from Blackpool and ending in Bournemouth, with 42 mainly Forestry Commission special stages completed over 2200 miles (3542km) – the fastest stage times were usually dominated by Scandinavian cars and drivers. This time, though, it was Tom Trana's Volvo PV544 that won the event, while Paddy's gallant Mini set fast times on 20 occasions. After such a gruelling event, when all the Minis suffered repeatedly from damage or breakages to the standard-type (rubber) drive shaft couplings, Paddy was delighted to take fourth place overall, while Logan Morrison won his class, too.

How could 1.1 litres of Mini Cooper S stay ahead of 4.2 litres of Ford Falcon Sprint on the Monaco GP circuit in 1963. Like this – in Casino Square – but only if Paddy Hopkirk was driving the Mini. This was 33 EJB's very first outing, where it took third place overall. (Reproduced from the BP/Castrol Archive)

Dirty weather, and very demanding stages, for Paddy Hopkirk in 8 EMO, a new 1071S, on his way to fourth in the 1963 RAC Rally. (Reproduced from the BP/Castrol Archive)

1964

If 1963 had been encouraging, this could not compare with what was to follow in 1964. Here, in summary, was a year which would see the launch of the definitive Mini Cooper – the 1275S – but there would also be outright victory for Paddy Hopkirk's 1071S on the Monte Carlo Rally, another outright win in the Tulip, and confirmation on all other occasions (and on the circuits too) that here was a quite remarkable little machine.

As in 1963, so in 1964 – early in the year everyone at Abingdon knew that two new derivatives of the Mini Cooper S – 970S and 1275S – were soon to be launched, though they were not allowed to let the public know in advance. In fact the new twins – one with a high-revving short-stroke engine, specifically developed for 1-litre circuit racing, one with the robust 1275cc engine – would be launched in March, and homologation followed within weeks. As already noted (in the 'Car and the Team' section), approval was gained by the famous 'smoke and mirrors' technique being practiced by all such 'works' teams at the time, and there do not seem to have been any complaints from rival manufacturers.

569 FMO, this 1071S, was used only once by the 'works' team – on the 1964 Monte, where Rauno Aaltonen took it to seventh place.

No rush, it seemed – but Paddy Hopkirk was on the final Monaco GP speed trial of the 1964 Monte Carlo Rally, just before confirming a famous victory.

As usual, BMC mounted a strong challenge on the Monte Carlo Rally, entering no fewer than six Minis. Four of those cars were 1071S-types – two of them (569 FMO and 570 FMO) being brand-new, the ex Tour de France car for Paddy Hopkirk, and the versatile and hard-worked 277 EBL for Pauline Mayman. Stuart Turner also provided a car for BBC Motoring Correspondent Raymond Baxter – not only because the publicity he brought to the team would certainly be welcome, but because he was already an accomplished and experienced rally driver.

As ever there was a performance handicap on this event, which slightly favoured smaller-engined cars, so BMC's big rivals from Ford-USA, using 4.7-litre Ford Falcon Sprints, would have to be substantially faster to gain official outright victory. Depending on the wintry weather conditions, the choice of starting points might be critical too – which maybe explains why the Minis started, variously, from Oslo, Minsk in Russia and from Paris.

To the victor, the spoils! After an event-long battle with the 4.7-litre Ford Falcon Sprint of Bo Ljungfeldt, Paddy Hopkirk (left) and Henry Liddon drove this 1071S – 33 EJB – to a narrow victory in the 1964 Monte Carlo Rally.

Paddy Hopkirk, Henry Liddon and their victorious 1071S, enjoying the pomp and ceremony of winning the 1964 Monte Carlo Rally. Prince Rainier and Princess Grace are on the podium.

The team had, of course, practiced assiduously – almost the entire fleet of 'works' Mini Coopers (there were few spare 1071S-types, of course – only 8 EMO as far as one can see!) being used from time to time, so all the drivers had detailed pace notes for the five special stages which would total nearly 110 minutes of flat-out motoring on the run down from Rheims to Monte Carlo. Although weather conditions on the road sections were much milder than in 1963 (163 of the 299 starters would finish), and there was little snow and ice on the stages, not even the 1071S cars could be fastest overall.

No sooner had 33 EJB won the 1964 Monte Carlo Rally, than BMC retired it, and used it as a show car for ever after. This study, dating from the 2000s, shows that in more than forty years it has never been modified or restored. Dunlop racing tyres used on the final circuit test in Monte Carlo are still fitted, and constant polishing has eroded some of the detail of the bonnet-mounted number plate.

As expected, the three A-team runners – Paddy Hopkirk, Rauno Aaltonen and Timo Makinen – were always among the front runners, with Paddy being marginally quicker than his Finnish team-mates. Unhappily, though, Pauline Mayman's car was hit by a non-competing car and badly damaged, breaking her leg and putting her out of rallying for several months. After a fabulous running battle with the big Fords (some of the stages, incidentally, were nicknamed 'Falcon Autobahns,' by the way), Paddy rolled into Monte Carlo, firmly in first place on handicap (from Ljungfeldt's Falcon), the Irishman making no mistake on the final Monaco GP circuit sprint which signalled the finale. At the end of the day, the fact that Paddy did not set one fastest time – he equalled the Falcon's stage time on one occasion – was swept aside by BMC's publicists.

It was Abingdon's very first Monte success, and one which secured Hopkirk's (and the Mini Cooper's) reputation for all time. The winning car – 33 EJB – was flown back to London, appeared on stage on the ITV show *Sunday Night at the London Palladium*, and millions knew all about the success.

Soon after this, in March, the 970S and 1275S derivatives were announced and, although production had only just begun, they were speedily homologated in April 1964. Just as soon as they could get their hands on rally-prepared 1293cc engines, Abingdon began to build up its fleet of 'works' 1275Ss – first being a quintet of cars registered AJB 33B, AJB 44B, AJB 55B, AJB 66B and BJB 77B. All would make their rally debut in the next three months.

Paddy Hopkirk's winning 1071S at Loews Hairpin on the Monaco GP circuit, just before winning the 1964 Monte.

Probably the most famous 'works' Mini Cooper S in the world? This was Paddy Hopkirk's Monte-winning car of 1964, pictured as soon as it returned from the rally, with all the lamps, rally plates and decals securely in place.

A place for everything and everything in its place – this was a mid-1960s (Morris-badged) Mini Cooper S fascia/instrument display.

Although the new 1275S was not the fastest car of all – on this event it could not keep up with the Morley twins' Austin-Healey 3000, or the Ford Falcon Sprint of Henri Greder – it was outstanding among other touring cars, particularly those with small capacity engines. For such a small saloon, not only was Timo's 1275S very fast – he totally dominated a class which included other Minis – but other Mini drivers including Julien Vernaeve (Group 3 Mini Cooper 1071S) and Brian Culcheth (1071S) also performed with great honour. As a result, BMC won the Manufacturers' Team Prize, too.

The team returned to Abingdon, now sure that they had the basis of a sensational rally car for the next few years. Because their driving team was already world class, and the team involved in engineering and preparing the cars was so talented, all they had to do (All? It would be a mammoth and continuing task!) was to squeeze yet more power out of the long-stroke engine, and make the rest of the car more reliable, and durable.

Not that this was going to be easy, as the team's next outing – to the rough, tough, hot and incredibly demanding Greek Acropolis Rally was to prove. The only previous Mini outings on the Acropolis had been with 850s in 1960 and 1961 (where two gallant but under-powered cars had finished, way down in 1960, but all three cars had retired in 1961), so this was bound to be an uphill battle.

Two cars took the start – AJB 33B for Rauno Aaltonen and AJB 55B for Paddy Hopkirk – and hopes were high, but

For the Tulip Rally, and because the class improvement handicap system was still in operation (which meant that, as the mathematicians realised, there was no point in putting a team of cars into the same capacity class), Abingdon prepared just one 'works' 1275S – which was AJB 66B, driven by Timo Makinen. Although this was a 1750 mile (2817.5km) event on tarmac roads, with only speed hill climbs and tests to sort out a result, loose-surface expert Timo loved his new car, attacked every challenge with great relish, and not only won his class, but won the Touring Category too. The result was that the brand-new car achieved outright victory, which vindicated Stuart Turner's and John Cooper's determination to get a 1.3-litre Cooper S out into motorsport as soon as possible.

both cars were forced to retire when very highly placed. Aaltonen's car had to retire with steering failure, while Hopkirk's car suffered similar problems and, only three hours from the finish, retired when a battery cable chafed through, causing an electrical short, immobilising the car.

It was wound-licking time for the 'works' team, yet only five weeks later (and in spite of a diversion to build an MGB to compete at Le Mans), four 'works' Mini Cooper S cars started the French Alpine Rally from Marseilles. Not only had Paddy Hopkirk's stricken ex-Acropolis car been recovered, and rebuilt, but two brand-new machines – AJB 44B and BJB 77B – appeared. All those ran as 1275cc-engined machines, but Pauline Mayman (her broken leg now mended) ran AJB 66B (Makinen's Tulip Rally mount) as a 970S, this being that model's rally debut.

Three of the cars ran in homologated Group 2 form, while Rauno's machine ran as a Group 3 'Grand Tourer,' modified to the extent of having aluminium doors, bonnet and bonnet lid. These items, incidentally, were not often used on the 'works' cars, and were kept stored 'in the rafters' of the workshops between outings.

In an event where the weather was very hot and dusty, and where target average speeds were high (this was done by the organisers quoting the length of sections as being much shorter than they actually were, and reducing time allowances accordingly – 'pruning' was alive and well on both sides of the English Channel in those days – which made this event something of a tarmac 'road race' on roads which were not closed to the public. No wonder, therefore, that Porsche supported the entry of 904s (which were really race cars) in the event …

Two of the 'works' cars had to retire – Timo's car broke down at an early stage, while Paddy Hopkirk's machine broke a suspension ball joint on the final leg – though Rauno Aaltonen and Pauline Mayman both won their class and won Coupes des Alpes for un-penalised runs on the road, with Rauno taking fourth overall in the GT category, behind an Alfa Romeo GTZ, the Big Healey of the Morleys and a Porsche 904. Although this was not quite as outstanding a result as Rauno had achieved in 1963, it was still a great performance by such a small car.

After another solid performance in the Finnish 1000 Lakes (Timo Makinen took fourth place overall in AJB 33B), BMC took a real gamble, by loaning an ex-Monte Carlo (Timo's car)/ex-practice car for John Wadsworth and Mike Wood to enter on the Spa-Sofia-Liège Marathon de la Route: there were six other 'works' cars – three Big Healeys and three MGBs. This extra-long, extra-tough, extra-tiring event was not for mere mortals, for it started from Spa in Belgium, going all the way to Sofia in Bulgaria, and returned to Liège in Belgium, with no overnight rest halts, and an almost impossible time schedule. Apart from a one-hour halt in Sofia, cars were on the go for more than 90 hours, non-stop, and few ever completed the course. Up to this point, no Mini had ever finished.

In 1964, not only did the intrepid Lancastrians virtually carry the battered old car round to the finish, but Rauno Aaltonen's 'works' Austin-Healey 3000 won the event outright. Only 20 out of the 98 starters actually made it to the end. The miracle was that the Mini Cooper kept going at all. Well before half distance, the Mini had deranged its sump shield, which was dragging on the ground, so this had to be lashed up to the bodyshell with a rope. On the return leg the crew was exhausted, and barely even able to keep awake but, although they were running last on the road, and needed to have the car's drive shafts changed (this was done by what became a time-honoured method, tipping the car on to its side so that the mechanics could get easier access!).

All of which must have made a four-car entry in the exceptionally long (3800 miles/6118km) Tour de France look like a positive holiday – though in its own way it was just as bruising, and just as exhausting, as the Liège had ever been. On this occasion, all four of the French Alpine cars (AJB 44B, AJB 55B, AJB 66B and BJB 77B) – BMC really did not have many spare rally cars at this stage – were re-prepared. Because the Tour was another event with a complex handicap-marking system which somehow always seemed to favour small-engined French cars, after reading the regulations the team decided to enter three of the cars as 970S-types, with only Rauno Aaltonen having a 'normal' 1275S.

After the great excitement which had built up at Abingdon, with victories in Monte Carlo, the Tulip and Spa-Sofia-Liège, the Tour was a great disappointment for all concerned, as three of the four cars retired. Compared with the Ford Mustangs, Jaguar MkIIs and Lotus-Cortinas which eventually dominated the Touring Car category, the high-revving 970S – 8000rpm for minute after minute at Le Mans, for instance – was always going to seem breathless. Three suffered a variety of mechanical maladies, though Pauline Mayman's car survived to win its class, and reach Nice. Running as a private owner in his 1275S, John Wadsworth also won his capacity class, so the event was not a complete write-off for BMC.

It had been the first time that Timo Makinen and Paul Easter had shared a rally car, so the oft-told story of how their 970S came to retire is well worth repeating: Approaching Grenoble on one of the final sections of the event, with Paul Easter at the wheel, the car swerved to avoid a kamikaze French taxi, and hit a kilometre post, badly damaging the suspension. According to Paul, Timo (who had been asleep, woke up, surveyed the wreckage, and immediately commented: 'I think we go find nice pub, and you buy me big drink …' There was, after all, little more that could have been said …

After this unhappy and expensive outing, the last event of the 'works' Mini's season was the British RAC Rally, where four 1275-types – two of them (CRX 89B and CRX 90B) – were brand-new, and where the team was hoping for a change of fortune. It was not to be, for although the

Clean, smart, and ready to take the start; this is Paddy Hopkirk and Henry Liddon starting the 1964 British RAC Rally. Clerk of the Course, Jack Kemsley, wields the Union Flag, John Gott is right behind him, and it is only 0700hrs. In honour of his Monte victory, Paddy carried Comp No One on this event – but it brought him no luck as the car retired.

cars were very competitive (three were in the top four positions at half-distance, at the night halt in Perth), all of them retired. On this occasion, and to take advantage of the regulations which applied, all three cars were run in Group 3 ('Grand Touring') condition, which meant that they could run non-standard in several respects.

Not that it helped. Harry Kallstrom led the event, then went out with a broken transmission differential, Carl Orrenius crashed AJB 44B (but things were about to change for that car, which would have a truly sensational run on the Monte that followed), Paddy Hopkirk went off the road, dropping 30 feet (9 metres) down a hill-side and stuck fast, while Rauno Aaltonen's gearbox casing broke when he was battling for the lead. The only solace was that Barrie Williams, driving his own 1.0-litre Mini Cooper, won his Group 2 capacity class, while a young Tony Fall won the 1300cc class in his employer's (Appleyards of Leeds) 1275S.

Mini Coopers in motor racing

The Mini Coopers and Cooper Ss also had a great career in motor racing. No sooner had the 997cc Mini Cooper been put on sale, than BMC hired the Cooper Car Co to race cars on its behalf in the British Saloon Car Championship. Recognisable from early days by their glossy green finish, and the two broad wide fore-aft stripes painted on the sides of the bonnet panel, in 1962 two cars (one driven by John Love, the other by Sir John Whitmore) dominated their 1-litre class, though Christabel Carlisle, driving a privately financed car which had been prepared by Don Moore, astonished everyone else with her pace and flair.

In 1962, John Love's 997cc car comfortably won his class many times, and no other 1-litre car could match its pace: accordingly, he became Saloon Car Champion. Although it was not quite the same story again in 1963 (Ford had latched on to the 'homologation special' business, producing the Lotus-Cortina), Sir John Whitmore used 997cc, then 1071cc, Minis to win his capacity class on most occasions, and took second in the Championship: Paddy Hopkirk backed him up all the way.

Things got even more serious in 1964. In Britain, although Ford rolled out a mass of Lotus-Cortinas (F1 World Champion Jim Clark drove one) and Galaxies, BMC now had the formidable 100bhp+ 1275S in the 1.3-litre class. Although Clark's Lotus-Cortina won several races outright, John Fitzpatrick's 1275S easily won the 1.3-litre category, and took second in the Championship.

Meanwhile, BMC hired Ken Tyrrell's team to run two works-supported Mini Cooper S-types in the European Saloon Car Championship, once again with an eye to winning their class, and taking best advantage of the favourable class marking position. Warwick Banks, John Rhodes and the Belgian driver Julien Vernaeve all drove them. The result was that Warwick Banks easily won his class and the European Championship. The Mini racing phenomenon was really on a roll.

After this, Abingdon's contracted teams found themselves coming under more and more pressure from 'homologation specials' which had been introduced by rival manufacturers: such cars, whether in the Mini Cooper classes or not, were always built with class domination in mind, and often had very different engines from their standard relatives.

For that reason, BMC (the cars being run by John Cooper) concentrated on the British series, with occasional forays to important overseas events. This explains why three 'works' cars were sent out to Sebring, in Florida, in March 1965, where Warwick Banks/Paddy Hopkirk (whose car had fuel feed problems) finished closely behind a class-winning ex-Broadspeed car.

In Britain, in 1965, the Cooper Car Co. cars were driven by John Rhodes (1300cc class) and Warwick

Banks (1000cc class), their main class opposition coming from the privately financed Broadspeed machines (driven by John Fitzpatrick and John Handley). After a ding-dong battle with the Superspeed 1.3-litre Ford Anglias, Rhodes won his Championship class, while Banks easily won the 1-litre category, and took second place overall in the series. This was a season, incidentally, when the Broadspeed cars sometimes proved to be faster than the Cooper Car Co. machines, which was embarrassing. The situation did not persist into 1966 as Broadspeed defected, to campaign Ford Anglias instead!

For 1966, and under pressure from several manufacturers, British Championship regulations changed considerably. Henceforth the racing would be under FIA Group 5 regulations, which was effectively 'free-formula,' the original bodyshell, and the original engine cylinder block had to be retained, but almost everything else could be changed. This meant that poorly-specified cars like the Ford Anglia Super could benefit enormously, while well-developed road cars like the 1275S had little to gain.

In the 1966 season, therefore, the 1300cc class featured a season-long points battle between John Rhodes's Cooper Car Co. 1275S, and John Fitzpatrick's 1-litre Broadspeed Ford Anglia. At the end of that year, both cars ended up with the same number of points, but the 1275S, still with a twin-choke Weber carburettor (instead of twin SUs) and about 120bhp from its Downton-tuned power unit, was clearly close to the peak of its development in that form.

By this time, Rhodes's driving methods, which seemed to be to ignore the brake pedal almost completely, to throw the car sideways before the corner, to lay a dense smoke screen from the spinning front wheels as he negotiated the corner, and to blind his rivals, was becoming legendary. Nothing that Dunlop could do would reduce the tyre smoke – but as Rhodes only wanted a cover to last for about one hour of racing, he wasn't at all worried about tyre wear …

A year later, Rhodes was retaining his mastery of the 1.3-litre class, helped along by the use of Lucas fuel-injection instead of a carburettor, though with the Group 5 Superspeed Anglias now developing about 145bhp this was beginning to be a real struggle. Even so, he triumphed by sheer consistency, won his capacity class, and took third overall in the Championship.

When BMC merged with Leyland Motors in January 1968, to form British Leyland, Abingdon could have had no idea of the huge impact it would have on their race and rallying activities. As noted elsewhere, British Leyland soon imposed a rationalisation programme, when it was made clear that all the corporation's marques – including Rover and Triumph – should be considered for future motorsport programmes.

Fortunately for Peter Browning, and the Cooper Car Co., by the time this edict was made clear, plans for the 1968 season were already in place. It was pure coincidence, however, that this was the year in which the 1275S was gradually overhauled by new opposition, principally from Ford. In 1969, with British Leyland's antipathy to competing anywhere in which they could not almost guarantee success, all 'works' programmes would be slashed. Instead of promoting rallying, up at Head Office, Lord Stokes's advisers made sure that Abingdon committed itself to racing, and rallycross, where the crowds were larger and the expenses were reduced.

Invented in the late 1960s to help TV fill its schedules on wet Saturday afternoons, rallycross – a cross between autocross (cars competing on loose surfaces on their own) and racing (small grids, on mixed surfaces) – had soon become very popular. Where traction and handling mattered, stripped-out 1275S-types driven by heroes like Hugh Wheldon and 'Jumping Jeff' Williamson soon became very popular.

As part of Lord Stokes' 'win where the public can see you doing it' policy, Abingdon was directed to enter cars in the ITV Winter series of 1968/1969. Handicapped by a total lack of preparation experience at first, the team provided John Rhodes and John Handley with ever-improving cars. The first victory came in April 1969, and, in the end, Rhodes's consistency provided second overall in the Championship series, but this was an experiment which was not repeated in the future.

In 1968, the Cooper Car Co. ran the 'official' 1275S race team (John Rhodes and Steve Neal were the drivers) in the British Saloon Car Championship, while there was also support for John Handley's British Vita-prepared 970S in the European Championship. Handley's experience allied to British Vita's preparation skills saw this friendly little team win its class, and due to the marking system, also win the European Championship outright.

For the Cooper Car Co, however, in the UK it was more of an uphill struggle. Even though they were now equipped with fuel-injected 1293cc engines, which produced about 130bhp, Rhodes and Neal had to fight a running battle with Broadspeed's 145bhp Escort GTs. If the Fords had been more reliable the battle would have been even tougher, but the good news for Abingdon was that John Rhodes once again won the 1.3-litre Championship class, and finished third overall in the series.

This, though, was the point at which Lord Stokes withdrew all financial support from contracted teams, and from Downton Engineering. Not only was the 'works'

team at Abingdon directed to go motor racing (a new art which it had to learn from scratch), but it also had to compete head-on with the now privately financed Cooper Car Co. team, which was re-born as Cooper-Britax-Downton.

Throughout 1969, John Rhodes and John Handley (Abingdon) fought head-to-head against Cooper-Britax-Downton (Gordon Spice and Steve Neal) and against the Broadspeed Escorts. Honours were split between the teams, with the most successful driver (Spice) finishing second in the 1.3-litre class. It took Abingdon until late summer to make up for a total lack of previous experience, but it all came right at the Austrian Salzburgring in October, when Rhodes and Handley took first and second overall in a tightly contested 1.3-litre race.

Amazingly, while all this brotherly fighting was going on, a private team, Equipe Arden, built up a new 8-port 970S, which produced phenomenal horsepower. Alec Poole concentrated on the British Championship, completely obliterated his opposition, and won the series outright. This, though, was the end of the classic Mini motor racing era – although ex-Downton engineer Richard Longman resurrected the layout in 1275GT form, to win the British Touring Series again before the end of the 1970s.

1965

BMC was now convinced that the 1275S, if made reliable, was a rally car which could win in almost any set of circumstances, and what was achieved in 1965 proved this in no uncertain manner. Not only would there be seven outright wins, but five of them were to be recorded by Rauno Aaltonen, who became European Rally Champion as a result. Tests and rally results now showed that it was often on a performance par with the Austin-Healey 3000s – 1.3 litres and front-wheel-drive matching 3.0 litres and rear-wheel-drive, quite remarkable. Not only that, but

in recent months a great deal of testing and development had been carried out with the new-fangled Hydrolastic suspension which, if truth be told, often seemed to give no improvement over the original 'dry' (rubber) suspension. However, since all Mini saloons had adopted Hydrolastic suspension from the autumn of 1964 (and this included the production-line Mini Cooper and Mini Cooper S models), the team was under great pressure to use such suspension in its new 'works' machines. As already noted, however, the changeover was by no means sudden, or complete – for 'dry' team cars continued to be used for a long time to come.

All such machinations, of course, took place during the winter of 1964/1965, while a phalanx of six snow/winter-spec 1275S-types were prepared for the Monte Carlo. Not only that, but there were to be two Austin 1800s as well. In fact this was almost an expensive failure for the team, but fortune sometimes shines on the brave. Only one of the team finished higher than 26th in general classification – but that was Timo Makinen, recording the most emphatic of victories which some observers (including his team boss, Stuart Turner) still call the rally epic of the century.

Forget about the failures, though, for the drama of this event – a story which no Hollywood scriptwriter could possible invent – was all about Makinen's epic drive. In an event where only 35 of the original 237 starters struggled through a blizzard to reach Monte Carlo, Makinen's Group 3-tuned 1275S was the only car in the event to be un-penalised on the road. Not only that, but he was much faster than anyone else on the eleven special stages – not slightly faster, but majestically faster. Eugen Bohringer's heroics in taking second place in a Porsche 904 should never be forgotten, but the fact is that Timo was 20 minutes (minutes, not seconds) faster than the Porsche in total.

An astute choice of tyres at all times (Dunlop had planned for every eventuality) certainly helped, as did BMC's meticulous planning and service support, but the genius was all that of the unbelievably talented Makinen. Incidentally, a great deal of luck was also involved for, as historian Bill Price has commented after the event:

"There was panic when the winning car would not start. The trouble was traced to the fibre insulating washer missing from the moving point in the distributor, left out when Paul and Timo had changed the points during the rally. It is a mystery why the car ran at all with this part missing …"

And so the legend was made.

The team then came down to earth with a bump in the Swedish Rally, when all four 1275S 'works' cars (two of them – DJB 92B and DJB 93B – being brand-new) retired with transmission differential failure, all apparently caused by the severe cold weather. Fortunately for team morale, a single car (CRX 89B – Rauno's ex-RAC Rally car from 1964) was made ready for Paddy Hopkirk to tackle his own Circuit of Ireland Rally, where he used the Mini's handling and his own experience to such good effect that he won the event outright.

Then came the Tulip Rally which, though held mainly in France and Germany at the end of April, will always be

In a performance often described as the 'drive of a lifetime,' Timo Makinen and Paul Easter used AJB 44B to pulverise their opposition in the 1965 Monte Carlo Rally.

remembered because it encountered fresh falling snow in the mountains around Geneva. Many cars simply failed to climb some of the passes along the way (the Col de la Faucille was one of these) but Timo Makinen kept going strongly in AJB 33B. Unhappily for him (and also for the Morley twins in the formidable fast Austin-Healey 3000), the special stage times were being assessed on the usual class improvement basis, so, although Timo was as fast as could have been hoped (the Big Healey was even faster), he was eventually classified as 'only' third overall, and won his class.

In what has often been described as the Drive of the Century, no-one could catch Timo Makinen's 1275S on its way to winning the 1965 Monte Carlo Rally. Strangely for an event beset with blizzards, there is no snow on the ground at this point.

The morning after the night before – Timo Makinen (right) and Paul Easter pose with AJB 44B, after their stunning drive to win the 1965 Monte Carlo Rally.

Paddy Hopkirk loved competing in his native Circuit of Ireland, particularly in 1275S-types, which were ideal for twisty tarmac stages. Using CRX 89B in much-modified form, and along with co-driver Terry Harryman, he won the 1965 event. (Reproduced from the BP/Castrol Archive)

Although he had to battle against an unfavourable performance handicap, Timo Makinen set a series of fast times in the 1965 Tulip Rally, to take third overall in the Touring Car category. (Reproduced from the BP/Castrol Archive)

To follow this, and only with reluctance, the team then entered a single Mini Cooper S in the Greek Acropolis Rally, not an event in which IT had previously been lucky, as the combination of rough roads, dust, high temperatures and high target average speeds was extremely demanding. This outing, in the end, was fruitless for, as Peter Browning later wrote:

"Sometimes you can retire from a rally quickly and painlessly … More often, however, one small mechanical difficulty leads to others until, finally, you are staggering around the route with the car slowly falling to pieces …"

And so it was, though the Mini had led the event for many hours until it finally lay down and died. First the exhaust system fell off (co-driver Paul Easter stowed it in the car), then a smell of burning told them that the carpets were on fire. Rubber drive shaft joints needed replacing while the car was on a ferry crossing (with the car tipped on its side …), then the rear sub-frame began to break up; the sump shield was holed … Later, there was a fire when the car was being welded while lying on its side, and a carburettor melted in the shortlived blaze; finally, the engine bearings seized. The entry of 'retired' in the lists hardly does justice to this catalogue of errors … Amazingly, this was a car (DJB 93B) which would be rebuilt, and in which Rauno Aaltonen would win the RAC Rally!

By comparison, Paddy Hopkirk's singleton entry in the Scottish Rally was positively incident-free, though on the same event it was quite over-shadowed by the bravura, but eventually fruitless, show put on by Timo Makinen in his 'works' Austin-Healey 3000. Paddy, for his part, battled and battled against the dust and temperatures of a near-tropical June in Scotland, but finally saw the Mini drop out with a broken transmission.

After this was one of the most remarkable runs of victory that the Mini Cooper S ever had – where team cars won six rallies outright, five of the wins going to Rauno Aaltonen. As a result, Rauno was crowned European Rally Champion, and deservedly so. Not only this, but it also confirmed the now-mature Mini Cooper S as Europe's most versatile and effective rally car – a Rally Giant by any standards.

First of all, there was the Geneva Rally, the usual brisk rush around the French mountains, special stages and hill climbs, which, as far as the Minis were concerned, was made all the more attractive by a performance handicapping system that slightly favoured small-engined

First identify your target … CRX 89B carried Comp No 3 in this shot, was on a forestry special stage, and running in much-modified condition. It was actually competing in the 1965 Scottish Rally, with Paddy Hopkirk driving, but was forced out with transmission failure.

No crowd control in Czechoslovakia in 1965, with Rauno Aaltonen on his way to victory in July 1965.

cars: Not that this sat well with the Morley twins in their 'works' Austin-Healey, which set the fastest overall scratch times, but were only rewarded by seventh place! Then came the Rallye Vltava in Czechoslovakia, when Rauno and Timo both started, but Timo retired. On that occasion, Rauno's car was brand-new, and had Hydrolastic suspension, the victory adding to his standings in the European Championship.

By comparison, Paddy Hopkirk's fine sixth place in the Nordrhein-Westfalen Rally (based on Cologne, in West Germany) was a great disappointment to him and the team, for on this event the performance handicap system did not favour his Mini Cooper S. Although either he, or Andrew Hedges ('works' MGB) won every special stage, the handicap knocked him back to sixth overall, and a class win, with outright victory going to – guess what? – a German Opel Kadett. Why was no-one surprised by this?

The French Alpine Rally which followed was, by comparison, a real challenge for true rally cars, which explains why BMC entered no fewer than five 'works' cars – four 1293cc-engined Mini Cooper S-types and one Austin-Healey 3000. This was the usual high speed thrash, with schedules set faster than ever, in which it was a real challenge to finish the event, and an almost (but not quite) impossible one to capture a Coupe des Alpes for an un-penalised run on the road sections.

According to the published results, Timo Makinen (using an old-type 'dry' suspension) took second place to Rene Trautmann's Lancia Flavia, only by the tiny margin of 1.7 seconds, but although Paddy Hopkirk took fourth, the other cars struggled a little, and Rauno Aaltonen suffered by being mis-directed at a road junction, by a French gendarme. Surely this cannot have been deliberate? Whatever, it cost Rauno his Coupe and therefore a possible Coupe d'Or (Gold Cup).

On the other hand, a brash young man called Tony Fall won his class in a privately entered car, and would soon become a regular 'works' team member. Among the favourable statistics were three Coupes – Timo, Paddy and Tony Fall – and a total of no fewer than 27 major trophies, while Paddy won a Coupe d'Argent (Silver Cup) for three non-consecutive Coupes des Alpes over the years.

More highlights followed, for Rauno went off to tackle the Polish Rally – another singleton entry – and fortunately this was an event which not only suited the Mini, but had several truly demanding and fast road sections on which Aaltonen excelled. Even though yet another much-hated handicap system was applied, the Mini rose above it, and won the event outright. For Rauno, that made it his third outright victory in two months …

Two 'works' Mini Cooper 1275Ss, and a Renault 8 Gordini, in line astern on a road section of the French Alpine Rally, 1965. Driving DJB 93B, Pauline Mayman was on her way to winning the Ladies' Award, while Timo Makinen, in AJB 33B, would win his class, and finish second in the Touring Car category. (Reproduced from the BP/Castrol Archive)

Another day, another Mini, another victory – and another brick in the wall on the way to the European Rally Championship for Rauno Aaltonen. Using CRX 89B, he won the Polish Rally in July 1965. (Reproduced from the BP/Castrol Archive)

Then came the Finnish 1000 Lakes, an event which the Mini Cooper S had yet to win. Determined to break this record, BMC therefore sent three cars for the 'A-team' to drive – Timo Makinen, Rauno Aaltonen and Paddy Hopkirk, all of them with local Finnish co-drivers. So confident in its cars by this time that, suitably refreshed of course, the same three cars which started the French Alpine were sent out to Finland to tackle another high speed event.

Perhaps it was a good omen too, for Timo was using the self-same car (or, at least, a car with the same registration number – AJB 33B!), with 'dry' suspension as in 1964, when he had finished fourth, and the same co-driver, which duly delivered the goods. Not only did Timo win the 'Finnish Grand Prix' outright, but Rauno took second place, and Paddy (who had never before tackled the event), finished sixth, highly delighted to have beaten many Finns on their own territory.

Then came the event which might just seal the European Championship for Rauno and BMC – the 'Three Cities,' a romantically-titled event which linked Munich (West Germany), Vienna (Austria) and Budapest (Hungary), all of which were grouped quite close together in Central Europe. Because team boss Stuart Turner was intent on supporting Rauno in every way, and to take advantage of a performance handicapping system, he made sure that two other crews (Tony Fall in AJB 55B and Geoff Halliwell in CRX 90B) should take part as private entries, specifically to help provide the best conditions. He also made sure that Paul Easter (in his own car) should enter, and should carry wheels and tyres, fuel, tools and spares for Rauno's car: it was a good ploy, ruined at the last minute when the organisers abandoned their 'no servicing' regulation …

Although this was not a demanding rally, the team enjoyed a very good run, Rauno won the event, Tony Fall finished second in class to him, though Geoff Halliwell unfortunately crashed out, injuring co-driver Mike Wood, who suffered concussion from which he soon recovered.

The last event of the BMC season, then, was to be the British RAC Rally, in which no fewer than five Mini Cooper S (and two Austin-Healey 3000s) took part. With Timo set to drive a Healey, Messrs, Aaltonen, Fall and Hopkirk led the Mini charge, along with Jorma Lusenius and Harry Kallstrom from Scandinavia. According to registration numbers, three of the Minis were old 1964 models, but they looked suspiciously new when seen at scrutineering on the day before the start in London! This was going to be a real marathon – London to Wales, to North Yorkshire, to Scotland, a night-halt at Perth, back to the Lake District, then down to Wales again, and finally to London. Not only were there to be 57 flat-out special stages totalling 500 miles (805km), but the weather forecast was for snow – and lots of it.

This well-known shot shows Rauno Aaltonen and Tony Ambrose jumping DJB 93B over the rough bridge in a Scottish special stage of the 1965 RAC Rally. On this event Rauno excelled himself, by defeating Timo Makinen's Austin-Healey 3000, mainly by having better traction on snowbound sections.

Cold, blustery, bleak weather – this was a special stage on the 1965 RAC Rally, where Tony Fall's 'works' 1275S was on its way to third in Class.

This is an event which has gone down into legend – not only because it was the only time that a Mini won the RAC Rally, but because it was only the wintry weather which foiled Timo Makinen's attempt to win the event in the Austin-Healey 3000. In the end, the results show that Rauno Aaltonen won the event outright in his Mini, DJB 93B, and that Makinen, who went off the road several times during the event, was leading until a very late stage on the return leg through Wales.

My own rally report in *Autocar* was headlined 'Weather? The Lot!,' which summed up an extraordinary week. Even so, Aaltonen's Mini drive was immaculate, and although he was not always fastest through the stages, he was always neat, tidy, rapid – and kept the car on the tracks. At half-distance, Makinen's Healey led, Rauno's Mini was second, with Kallstrom's car fourth and Lusenius's machine eighth – all other works cars having wilted, or suffered from hold-ups on stages, or suffered from transmission or suspension problems. In the end, Rauno beat Makinen's Healey by more than three minutes, while Jorma Lusenius took sixth place, 29 minutes behind.

This was a phenomenal end to an amazing season, for the Mini Cooper S had now emphasised that it was Europe's most versatile, successful and popular rally car.

1966

Although it was expecting too much for BMC's 1966 season to be as sensational as it had been in 1965 – there was no slackening in the cars' progress: indeed, without the controversies which are to be described below, there might have been even more outright victories than before. However, although the 'works' Mini Cooper S eventually won eight major rallies (two of them in Great Britain), it was also embroiled in a scandal in Monte Carlo and a most unsavoury protest drama in the Acropolis. The Mini Cooper S, it seemed, had almost come to the peak of its influence in rallying, and the opposition was clearly not at all happy about that.

In the New Year, the team's first task was to cope with the abrupt change of regulations which had been imposed by the Monte Carlo Rally organisers and, in particular, to make sure that the 1275S was re-homologated into Group 1 form. Because more than 5000 cars had genuinely been produced in 1965, this was done without drama.

Preparation of cars at Abingdon, ahead of the 1966 Monte. GRX 55D is Rauno Aaltonen's brand-new Group 1 car, while that carrying competition No 87 is GRX 195D, to be driven by Raymond Baxter.

For the 1966 Monte, the organisers promoted to impose a swingeing handicap on Group 2 and Group 3 cars, so BMC were virtually obliged to enter three brand-new showroom standard cars (GRX 5D, GRX 55D and GRX 555D), though a fourth brand-new car (GRX 195D) was entered for BBC Motoring Correspondent Raymond Baxter. Every serious factory team also prepared Group 1 cars, so the playing fields, as they say, were level once again. Behind the scenes, and spoken very softly, however, it was widely suggested that the organisers 'intended' that the event would be won by a French car, and that they intended to make sure, by hook or by crook, that this happened …

Because 'standard' meant that standard seats had to be used, along with no more than two auxiliary driving lamps, these cars were little more special than those to be found in any BMC showroom. However, because the team was using the new-fangled Lucas single-filament quartz-halogen headlamp bulbs, it had been arranged for the dipping action to transfer the lights to those auxiliary lamps.

On the road, Rauno Aaltonen took second place in the 1966 Monte Carlo Rally (behind team-mate Timo Makinen's car) – but the scrutineers disqualified him on a ludicrous lighting technicality.

Rear view of Paddy Hopkirk's Group 1 1275S on the 1966 Monte.

In 1966 the 'works' Mini Cooper 1275S-types beat everyone else on the Monte Carlo Rally, but were then disqualified by post-event scrutineering controversy. Here, an official points out the lighting system which caused so much controversy.

The story of this event is easily told (and has been analysed thousands of times since the event took place). As in 1964 and 1965, the Minis dominated the event: careful practice, detailed pre-event reconnaissance, extensive 'ice-notes' preparation and a wide choice of tyres all helped to make them ideal for the event, the result being that they finished 1-2-3 (Makinen, Aaltonen and Hopkirk) – but were then disqualified! Although everyone except the organisers was convinced that the team had been stitched up in a dispute over the headlamp/dipping arrangements, this did not help, and 'victory' was awarded to – guess what? – a French Citroën instead.

BMC's only consolation was that it probably reaped more publicity from this farrago than if it had been granted its rightful victory. Incidentally, the 'winner' (Pauli Toivonen) refused to attend the prize-giving ceremony and swore that he would never again drive for Citroën: the world of rallying completely backed him over this firm stand.

It then took time for the BMC team to recover its spirits. First of all, the two Finns were sent off to contest the Swedish Rally, where both Group 2 cars retired – one with overheating after a rock smashed the cooling radiator, the other with a broken drive shaft – after which Paddy Hopkirk and Tony Fall started the Italian Flowers Rally, where Paddy's car suffered engine overheating and repeated punctures, while Fall's (ex-Hopkirk/Monte Carlo) Group 1 car was disqualified after he was found to be running without an engine air filter element in place.

Then the team's fortunes changed. First of all, Paddy and Tony Fall tackled the Circuit of Ireland, where Tony Fall recorded his first outright victory for the team, and only days later the two Flying Finns tackled the Tulip which, for the first time in years, was being run off without a class handicapping system of any type. Not only did the Minis therefore get to compete in level competition (and, even against Porsches, they were competitive!), but Rauno Aaltonen used a Group 2 car (GRX 310D) to win outright, while Timo Makinen used an ex-Monte Group 1 car to win the Group 1 category outright.

Paddy Hopkirk then made a happy return to Austria for the Austrian Alpine Rally, which he had won in 1964 in a 'works' Austin-Healey 3000. This time he was in DJB 93B (the car which Rauno had used to win the 1965 RAC Rally), and in spite of a very stringently-policed 'no-service' regulation he managed to win again. The fact that he managed to get adequate sub-rosa service support from Bill Price and a small team was reflected in the strategies operated by other teams, including the 'works' Porsches – so honour was satisfied.

The only people in the motoring world who did not think that Timo Makinen and Paul Easter had won the 1966 Monte Carlo Rally were the post-event scrutineers, who seemed determined to find a flaw – any flaw, no matter how trifling – in the specification of this Group 1 1275S.

Top and bottom: BBC Motoring's Correspondent, Raymond Baxter, was sometimes invited to drive 'works' Minis – in this case taking charge of a fully-modified, Group 2 1275S, GRX 195D, on the 1966 Monte Carlo Rally. On this occasion his co-driver was Jack Scott (who was once Paddy Hopkirk's co-driver). Like other team cars, he was disqualified for spurious headlamp 'irregularities' – the organisers have never lived down that scandal.

On only its second
event – the first had
been in Sweden, where
the transmission failed
– GRX 310D was driven
to outright victory in
the 1966 Tulip Rally by
Rauno Aaltonen. This
shot was taken on a
military training ground
not far from the finish in
Holland. (Reproduced
from the BP/Castrol
Archive)

Built brand-new for the
1966 Monte, where it fell
foul of the organisers'
disqualification strategy,
GRX 5D was still a Group
1 car when driven by
Timo Makinen in the
1966 Tulip Rally. Timo
won his capacity class,
and was also a member
of the winning team.
(Reproduced from the
BP/Castrol Archive)

In one of his finest-ever drives, Rauno Aaltonen took GRX 310D to outright victory in the Tulip Rally of 1966. Not even Vic Elford's 'works' Ford Lotus-Cortina could keep up with him.

Then came the Acropolis – a high profile rough-road event which BMC so dearly wanted to win – but as it transpired it would have to wait for another year to achieve that. Every team looked on an Acropolis victory as being as important as victory in the Safari – the prestige of the contest was that high – so BMC had prepared well, and at length. Three Hydrolastically-suspended Group 2 cars – GRX 311D, HJB 656D and JBL 172D – were brand-new for the occasion, and were as near to being little 'ten-foot tanks' as Abingdon could make them, for the 'A-Team' to drive.

It was just as well that they were new, as all three cars took a tremendous battering, and suffered from the heat and the dust. Of the cars, Rauno's retired with engine trouble, while Timo's broke a rear suspension bracket, and blew a head gasket on the very last speed test at the Tatoi airfield near Athens. Paddy's car somehow kept going, but had to be patched up at regular intervals, and beat all the 'works' Fords and other competitors, and was provisionally acclaimed as winner.

Then, just minutes before the end of the hour long 'protest' period, a protest saw Paddy penalised for 'illegal' servicing 'within a control area' earlier in the rally, and though this was certainly a trumped-up charge, it was upheld: the result was that Paddy was pushed back to third place – and BMC was furious. Appeals were swept aside. Who protested? Ford, it seemed – and it was one of its 'works' Lotus-Cortinas which benefitted …

Could the season get worse? Not except for the normal misfortunes of rallying, it seemed, as the next few events proved. First of all, Tony Fall was dispatched to tackle a very hot and dusty Scottish Rally, which he won with consummate ease, after which he flew off to tackle the Geneva Rally, which he contested in EBL 56C (which had been reborn as a Group 1 car), and took a very brave and talented second place overall, close behind Gilbert Staepelaere's 'works' Lotus-Cortina.

Tony then returned to 'borrow' DJB 93B to tackle the gruelling Gulf London Rally, which he led convincingly until the last morning, when he rolled the car into scrap after bouncing over a bumpy, abandoned, railway crossing. Since the organisers had not marked this as a hazard, Tony was not best pleased – and neither was co-driver Mike Wood, who observed the Mini's low-flying antics from close quarters!

Then came a further rush of success – first of all in the Czech Rally (Rauno Aaltonen, JBL 494D, another brand-new car for

No space, surely, for any more instruments, clocks, dials or switches in this well-equipped Group 2 'works' Mini? This car was badged as a 'Morris,' but on its next event it might equally be badged as an 'Austin' …

By 1966 BMC was so busy that it occasionally gave works support to well respected private owners driving their own cars. This was Lars Ytterbring of Sweden, in his own car, on the Scottish Rally. Second overall behind Roger Clark's 'works' Lotus-Cortina was a fine result.

It tells us how much was expected of the 'works' Minis that third overall in France, and second overall on the RAC were both regarded as failures by the team.

All four of BMC's regularly contracted drivers used fully-tuned Group 2 cars (85bhp at the front wheels) to tackle the French Alpine – as usual, held in high summer, in hot weather, mainly in the mountains between the Mediterranean and Geneva – but although they were competitive, three cars went out with a blown engine, broken differential and a lost wheel. Only Rauno Aaltonen, that most feline of drivers, made it to the finish in JBL 495D, third overall behind an Alfa Romeo GTA and Roger Clark's 'works' Lotus-Cortina: if only his car had not suffered a mysterious electrical failure close to the end, he might have pipped the Ford.

For the RAC Rally, Stuart Turner clearly decided to 'get rid of the empties,' for no fewer than eight 'works' Minis took the start, including a car for F1 World Champion Graham Hill, who was accompanied by Maxwell Boyd of *BBC Wheelbase/The Sunday Times*. This, of course, was the event in which F1 star Jim Clark also competed – and crashed – in a 'works' Lotus-Cortina, which seemed to soak up most of the newspaper headlines.

In summary, four of the cars retired, or were crashed (Simo Lampinen), while three of the survivors finished second (Kallstrom), fourth (Aaltonen) and fifth (Tony Fall). Timo Makinen – guess who? – led the event for nearly three days, but his car finally died in Keilder with a worn-out engine and broken transmission: the author had the pleasure of giving him a lift back to civilisation …

that occasion), then in the Polish Rally (Tony Fall, using GRX 309D, but with a 970S engine, to run in the 1-litre class and take advantage of a favourable handicap), and then the Finnish 1000 Lakes event, where Timo, Rauno and Jorma Lusenius were determined to repeat their 1965 'whitewash.' And so it was. Timo had won in 1965, and did so in 1966, while Rauno had finished second in 1965, and third in 1966.

Although Timo would then win the Three Cities – Munich-Vienna-Budapest – in October, the season ended with two major events – the French Alpine and British RAC – where, by BMC standards, the results were disappointing.

Timo Makinen and Paul Easter, in clouds of thick dust, on their way to victory in the 1966 Three Cities (Munich-Vienna-Budapest) Rally. This 'works' car would end its career on the 1967 East African Safari.

Timo Makinen on his way to winning the Munich-Vienna-Budapest Rally of 1966.

On one of his rare outings for the factory team, Simo Lampinen of Finland drove JBL 495D on the 1966 RAC Rally. No fewer than eight 'works' cars started this event, with Harry Kallstrom highest placed, in second.

Paddy Hopkirk and Ron Crellin in JMO 969D, on a Scottish special stage of the 1966 RAC Rally, the first to be sponsored by *The Sun* newspaper. Their hard-working 1275S eventually retired with a broken drive shaft coupling.

1967

Two things dominated the atmosphere at Abingdon in the opening weeks of the new season. One was that Stuart Turner was about to leave his post as Competitions Manager – to be replaced by Peter Browning – and the other was that the entire organisation was plotting revenge for the Monte Carlo Rally fiasco of 1966. Peter has often said that initially he felt quite incapable of replacing Stuart Turner – but did so, after a rousing talking-to from MG general manager John Thornley – but the team was convinced that it could win the Monte. In January 1966, the attitude had been 'we wuz robbed,' and that atmosphere persisted for a full year.

For 1967, the Monte organisers imposed an 'eight tyres per leg' rule, which meant that every driver had to nominate his tyres in advance, all had to be marked, and all had to be carried aboard throughout. Not only did BMC arrange to carry two spares in the boot, and two on special mountings in the rear passenger compartment, but the team also homologated new-type magnesium-alloy Minilite wheels. BMC entered five cars, four of them being brand-new – these being registered LBL 6D, LBL 66D, LBL 606D and LBL 666D, the fifth being Timo's ex-Three Cities-winning machine from 1966.

The third of the brand-new 'LBL … D' cars to tackle the 1967 Monte Carlo Rally was driven by Paddy Hopkirk and finished sixth overall.

Rauno Aaltonen's 1275S in full flight in a special stage of the 1967 Monte Carlo Rally. In this shot, the Perspex covers over the headlamps have both been unclipped, and are flying loose.

As it happened, the team's determination, to make amends, was fully justified. Four out of the five cars finished, and although there was a formidable challenge on all the special stages, from Vic Elford's Porsche 911S and a fleet of 1.3-litre engined Lancia Fulvia HFs, Rauno Aaltonen came home the narrow winner (by 13 seconds, from Ove Andersson's Lancia), while Paddy Hopkirk took a brave sixth place, with Tony Fall tenth. The only cloud was cast by a mysterious accident which befell Timo Makinen's car on the final night, when he was fighting for the lead – high in the mountains, his car suddenly struck a large boulder which 'accidently' fell into his path, thus wiping out the distributor, starter motor and oil cooler. Sabotage? For sure, but the culprits were never found.

Before encountering the notorious rock which just happened to be in the road in front of them on a special stage, Timo Makinen and Paul Easter led the 1967 Monte Carlo Rally for many hours.

Calm before the storm – on the concentration run in towards Monte Carlo on the 1967 event, Henry Liddon drives LBL 6D, with Rauno Aaltonen taking a nap. That year, because of regulations, extra wheels and tyres were sometimes carried on removable roof racks. Another 'works' Mini – probably that of Simo Lampinen in Comp No 178 – follows close behind.

Never had revenge been so sweet. This was Stuart Turner's last Monte Carlo in charge, so it was good to go out on a high note. Victory for Rauno made it three (and it should have been four) Monte wins for the Mini Cooper S, one each by each of the team's star drivers – and it was a great start to the season. That, as we will now see, was to be eventful – and successful.

Anything that happened in the next few months must surely have been

HJB 656D had an eventful life in 1966 and 1967. Simo Lampinen drove it on the Monte Carlo Rally of 1967 – seen here on the run to the Principality, with all driving lamps padded over, and extra spare wheels on the roof rack.

In 1967 Rauno Aaltonen, Henry Liddon and LBL 6D achieved a famous victory in the Monte Carlo Rally. This was a road section, not far from the Mediterranean, which explains the lack of crash helmets.

considered an anti-climax, though Rauno Aaltonen did his best to confound that by rolling his car on the Swedish Rally, losing most of his personal documents out of a disappearing rear window, and finishing third overall, while Paddy Hopkirk only achieved second in the Flowers Rally (using a brand-new car, LBL 590E) by being pushed down hill to the final control by a 'works' service car! A drive shaft had broken at the end of the final special stage, and could not have been replaced in the time available – although other crews suspected what happened, there were no final complaints, and his place stood.

Up until the last night, Timo Makinen was leading the 1967 Monte Carlo Rally. Then his Mini hit a large boulder which had been placed in the road by vandals. (Reproduced from the BP/Castrol Archive)

Paddy Hopkirk and Ron Crellin took sixth place in the 1967 Monte Carlo Rally. Icy roads, some snow on the verges, and bitterly cold conditions were all typical of this event.

Next on the list was what really qualified as a joke entry – Rauno Aaltonen drove a Group 2 1275S in the East African Safari – an event where track conditions, allied to ten-inch wheels and limited ground clearance, made it almost pointless to start. Rauno, however, had been awarded a free entry in the Safari when he won the 1965 RAC Rally, and thought it might be good fun to try.

HJB 656D, which had already tackled four major events (Simo Lampinen had recently driven it in the 1967 Monte) was chosen, and was made as special as possible, not only by having a hand-operated Hydrolastic pump mounted in the back seat area to raise the ride height if possible, but also with lifting handles on the front wings, and on the rear corners of the roof, to help 'volunteers' lift it out of the mud if necessary. The only nod to economy, and practicality, was that Minilite wheels were not included – the normal (and cheaper!) steel wide-rim wheels being used instead.

It was all to no avail, however, for the car suffered from engine overheating, and from dust ingress into the engine via inadequate carburettor air filters. Though fruitless, it must have been a pleasant way to spend the Easter weekend, as was Paddy Hopkirk's visit to his native Ireland, where he won the Circuit of Ireland outright in GRX 5D, that car's only victory.

What followed, between May and September, was then a full and final flowering of the Mini at its best. Not only would outright victories be recorded in the Acropolis, the Geneva, the 1000 Lakes and the French Alpine, but a 1275S came close to beating Vic Elford's Porsche 911S in the Tulip, and to winning the monumentally exhausting 84-Hour

Marathon at the Nürburgring. No-one, surely, could ever have expected more than this?

At this stage of its career, all that the 1275S now lacked was outright performance – for on tarmac the cars could often not keep up with the Porsche 911s, or with the ever-improving Alpine-Renault A110s. Now that Hardy Spicer drive shaft joints had replaced the original rubber-type, transmission reliability was much improved, but there was always a danger that the engines might over-heat, this depending on a whole raft of minor details; how 'tight' the originally-built engine had been, whether it was a slow or a fast rally, and whether the ambient temperature was high or low. Suffice to say that engine overheating could be just as much of a problem in 1967 and 1968, as it had ever been in earlier years.

The author took this picture of Rauno Aaltonen's 'works' Mini Cooper S before the start of the 1967 Safari Rally. Within hours it would fall foul of the awful conditions of the East African climate.

HJB 656D had already enjoyed a busy 'works' career before BMC kitted it out for Rauno Aaltonen to use in the 1967 Safari Rally. Among the special fittings were lifting handles on the front wings and on the rear of the roof structure (in case the little car got stuck in deep mud), a blank over the front grille to keep out mud, and inside a special Hydrolastic 'pump-up' installation to keep the car at the appropriate ride height.

Three cars, two of them brand-new for Timo and Rauno, turned up at the start of the Tulip Rally (which no longer applied any handicapping formula to stage times), the third being for David Benzimra of Nairobi. As ever, the Tulip was decided by a series of tarmac-surfaced speed hill climbs where Vic Elford's Porsche was unbeatable, but the two Finns both drove their heart out to keep him in sight. Although the engine in Timo's car was sick from a early stage (a broken piston ring was suspected, after which the engine misfired and consumed gallons of Castrol) he still keep going very fast, eventually winning the entire Touring Car category, with Rauno Aaltonen just 11 seconds behind.

Only weeks later, BMC gained its second revenge of the year, when Paddy Hopkirk (in another brand-new car, LRX 830E) won the Acropolis Rally. In contrast to 1966, there was no skulduggery over 'illegal' servicing, or last-minute protests, and the gallant little car survived all the dust, the temperature and the rocks to beat the massed ranks of the Ford and Lancia teams. Rauno Aaltonen crashed out when he hit a non-competing car coming the wrong way up a stage, while Makinen's car broke a sub-frame and had to retire. Paddy's luck was in, though. He was so far ahead before the final race at Tatoi airfield could begin, that when the engine bearing broke up during the race, he simply switched off near the finishing line, and eventually motored across the line when the 30 minutes were up!

After Lars Ytterbring's 'works' 1275S had finished second to Roger Clark's Lotus-Cortina in Scotland, Tony Fall and Julien Vernaeve were then sent off to tackle the Geneva Rally. The regulations were written so that effectively there were two events taking place at the same time, and although Elford's Porsche was much quicker than the Minis, they were theoretically in a different rally, and won their category quite convincingly –

finally, that is, for at one time Sandro Munari's Lancia Fulvia HF was leading them on absolute times.

Time for a summer break? Not for Abingdon, for sure. No sooner had Tony Fall returned from Switzerland than he 'borrowed' GRX 5D (which had retired in the Scottish) to use in the Gulf London Rally where, in theory, genuinely assisted 'works' cars were not allowed. This poor battered car (it had had a difficult time in the Scottish) suffered more in the long and exhausting London, so much so that it gradually started breaking suspension and structural pieces, and after Tony had also been off the road in Wales, it lay down and died. Amazingly, GRX 5D would be reborn two months later – as a light-weight Group 6 for the Nürburgring Marathon – and you still believe in registration numbers?

All the drama of night-time rallying in the mid-1960s, this being guest driver David Benzimra, along with Terry Harryman, on the 1967 Tulip Rally.

After Rauno Aaltonen had been forced out of the Danube Rally at the Hungarian border for not having an appropriate visa (he was leading the event at the time), Abingdon's attention turned to the 1000 Lakes where just one car (GRX 195D, which had suffered much on the Acropolis Rally) was made ready for Timo Makinen: Even at this stage, and three years after Hydrolastic suspension had been standardised on new Cooper S road cars, Timo's car was still running with the 'dry' rubber setup. BMC's sales division was never happy with this on-going situation, but were happy to accede – just so long as the cars were still winning.

In Finland, no question, Timo was quite determined to win, and after a running battle against 'works' Lotus-Cortinas and Saab V4s, did just that. Although his car suffered from engine overheating – there was never going to be a definitive cure for this problem on the fully-tuned rally cars – and there was one case where the bonnet panel flew up at high speed after a service check, it was only a broken gearbox remote control housing which looked like stopping the car in its tracks: in the end, Timo won by just eight seconds (from Simo Lampinen's Saab V4) and completed a hat-trick of 1000 Lakes successes.

Rauno Aaltonen and LRX 829E pushing on to third overall in the 1967 Tulip Rally. Minilite wheels had become the usual 'works' equipment by this time.

Belgian driver Julien Vernaeve was on the fringes of the 'works' BMC team in the 1960s. Here, he rallies his own privately-prepared 1275S in the 1967 Tulip Rally: with Mike Wood as his co-driver, he was a member of the winning Manufacturers' team, and took fourth overall in the Touring Category.

had 'won' the 1967 Acropolis Rally), such niceties were only for the naive.

These new 970S race cars both had lightweight bodies, aluminium panels, and auxiliary forward-facing cooling radiators, but ran with Group 2 engines: in each case, three drivers were nominated for each car. Running to a pre-determined plan, the event started gently for BMC, but after 12 hours the cars held down third and fourth places. After more than two days – the event really was that long – Alec Poole crashed one of the cars in thick fog, and although the surviving Mini held the lead for some hours late in the event, it was eventually overhauled by the Elford/Herrmann/

Next came an entry in the 84-Hour Marathon de la Route race/endurance rally around the Nürburgring circuit in Germany. In 1966 BMC had entered MGBs, and won the event outright, so the new team boss Peter Browning was already very familiar with the complex regulations. A study of what was proposed for 1967 convinced him that Group 6 (prototype-spec.) 970S-types would be most suitable, so two new cars were prepared. Although both registration numbers were familiar (GRX 5D had been on the car used by Paddy Hopkirk to win the recent Circuit of Ireland, and LRX 830E

On this rare occasion in 1967, Abingdon prepared two ultra-special 970S race cars, in Group 6 condition, to contest the 84 Marathon de la Route at the Nürburgring. In a fabulous performance with what was effectively a brand-new car (don't be fooled by the registration plate!), Tony Fall, Julien Vernaeve and Andrew Hedges took second overall – to a Porsche 911. (Reproduced from the BP/Castrol Archive)

Neerpasch Porsche 911S, and had to settle for second place. In 84 hours it had completed 5460 miles (8790.6km) – only 13 cars finished the event.

Then came the French Alpine Rally, which had scrapped all handicaps, and whose target average speeds were the highest ever, an event which goes down in history as one of the most demanding rallies ever held in this golden age. Because the regulations allowed it, Abingdon built up three Group 6 (prototype) cars for Aaltonen, Makinen and Hopkirk, plus a Group 2 car for Tony Fall. The Group 6 machines not only had light-alloy and fibreglass panels, but Perspex side and rear windows, no bumpers, and were fitted with single twin-choke Weber carburettor-type engines, plus an auxiliary front cooling radiator. Not only did they

Minilite wheels with centre-lock fixings were finally used for the first time on the 1967 Tour de Corse. GRX 5D was trying out these wheels in pre-event testing.

A famous picture, but worth reusing – Timo Makinen at the wheel, Tony Fall alongside him (later, he admitted to being terrified). GRX 311D was one of the highly-tuned Group 6 cars which BMC had prepared for the 1967 RAC Rally. That event was cancelled due to the foot-and-mouth disease outbreak, so cars took part in a TV spectacular instead.

produce 90bhp as measured at the front wheels, but were at least 110lb/50kg lighter than a Group 2 machine.

Although the team realised that they would be battling with other outright racers, such as Alpine-Renault A110s, Porsches and Alfa Romeo GTAs, they hoped that reliability would make up for this. Unhappily, Tony Fall crashed his car on the first day, Rauno's car broke its gearbox, and Timo Makinen's car began to suffer from engine overheating. Although Timo moved up to second place, he dropped out with brake problems and eventually idler gear failure, and it was not until the final hours that Paddy Hopkirk took the lead, eventually to beat Bernard Consten's Alfa GTA by almost ten minutes. Paddy was quite exhausted by this, but it was a satisfying win in an event which suited the 1275S so well.

If the season had reached its high note with Paddy Hopkirk's victory in the French Alpine, then it ended with farce in the Tour de Corse, where two Group 6 cars started the event, but both cars retired within a few miles when they

suffered from badly slipping fan belts, which led the engines to overheat. A faulty batch of belts was diagnosed.

The team might then have found solace in the British RAC Rally, where four Group 6 (prototype specification) cars had been prepared with fuel-injected 1293cc engines. However, due to the continuing spread of bovine foot-and-mouth disease throughout England and Wales, which meant that the route had to be repeatedly truncated, the event was cancelled on the evening before the start. All that could be run was a 'TV special' event in a forestry stage close to London, where Timo Makinen drove GRX 311D. This was no substitute for the real thing …

1968

Quite suddenly, it seemed, the pace of the Mini Cooper rally programme eased off in 1968. Compared with 1967, when the 'works' team had started 15 events (and won six of them), there would only be nine starts and, unfortunately, not a single victory. It was not that the Mini bubble had burst, but that the opposition, and major corporate events had caught up with them.

In summary, not only had the Porsche 911 and Alpine-Renault A110 matured into excellent, reliable, rally-winning machines, but Ford launched the new Escort Twin-Cam. Not only had Abingdon's parent company, BMC, been subsumed into the new British Leyland colossus, but a combination of corporate pressure and sporting realities led to huge, time-consuming and costly diversions, into sending BMC 1800 models into the Safari, and into the inaugural London-Sydney Marathon. Although the 1968 'works' Minis were better than ever before, so, too, were their rivals …

Once twin fuel tanks, a spare wheel/tyre, and various other gear had been stowed in the boot, there was no spare space. What car and when? This was ORX 707F, a 1968 'works' car which made its debut on the Monte Carlo Rally. The weird spanners are for loosening centre-lock Minilite wheels – which, in fact, were not used on the Monte.

As ever, the season started with a big effort in the Monte Carlo Rally – the biggest Mini effort of the year, as it transpired – where Abingdon prepared four brand-new cars for the occasion: ORX 7F, ORX 77F, ORX 707F and ORX 777F. Was the '7' significant? My guess was that this was a subliminal way of celebrating the start of the seventh year of Mini Cooper competition (the car had been homologated in January 1962 and had already completed six busy seasons): this, too, would be the seventh occasion in which a Mini Cooper had started the Monte …

The story of the 1968 Monte has often been told, for it was another of those occasions where the 'works' Minis and the Monte organisers seemed to be at cross-purposes throughout: there is no doubt in the author's mind that the Monegasques were thoroughly irritated by the way that the Mini Cooper S had bounced back from the shambles of the 1966 event to win in 1967, and they were always on the look out for infringements (real or imagined) that BMC had made in cars to be entered in 'their' event.

As already noted, Group 2 engines prepared for the 1968 Monte were very special, for special Weber carburettors had been mated to un-modified inlet manifolds to liberate more power (up to 93bhp at 6500rpm, as measured on the rolling road – close to race car figures, and about 6bhp more than normally recorded by a 'works' rally car …). Although this was within the Appendix J Group 2 regulations, the organisers tried to see it otherwise, and initially threatened all manner of penalties. In the end, they backed down, a rather tense stand-off was reached, and the Minis competed unchanged.

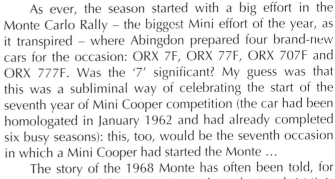

Paddy Hopkirk and Ron Crellin on a non-competitive section (no crash helmets!) of the 1968 Monte Carlo Rally. ORX 777F was brand-new for this occasion, and would finish fifth overall. Note the Minilite wheels, which had been homologated in 1967.

Just a few moments' rest at a BMC service point on the 1968 Monte Carlo Rally. Driver Rauno Aaltonen talks to Geoff Mabbs (providing 'ice notes' information, perhaps?), Henry Liddon relaxes, while mechanic Den Green works on the front of the car.

Explanations, please? How is a 1964 'works' Mini following a 1968 'works' Mini on the 1968 Monte? Because Tony Fall (in ORX 707F – he finished fourth overall) is ahead of Denis Cresdee (who had bought DJB 92B when its 'works' career was over at the end of 1966).

By 1968 the 'works' Minis were virtually at their peak, most of them running with Hydrolastic suspension, and all of them now using Minilite wheels – Rauno Aaltonen and Henry Liddon in full flight ...

Because they had won the Monte Carlo Rally in 1965, Timo Makinen and Paul Easter started near the front, No 7, in 1968. Clear tarmac on the Monte was a rare privilege – this, the author thinks, being the lower reaches of the Levens hillclimb, close to Nice.

ORX 7F was brand-new for Rauno Aaltonen to drive in the 1968 Monte Carlo Rally with Henry Liddon as his co-driver. After a fine drive, he took third place.

A combination of mild weather and a stupendous performance by Vic Elford's 'works' Porsche 911 saw the 'works' Minis pushed down to third, fourth and fifth places (they not only won their class, but the Manufacturers' Team Prize too …) in order Aaltonen-Fall-Hopkirk, though Timo Makinen had to retire when his engine threw a crankshaft pulley and immediately overheated.

Two of those cars – 77F and 777F – were immediately re-prepared for the Italian Rally of the Flowers (an event which, of course, became the San Remo in later years). Both cars retired with mechanical bothers, but few people noticed as this was the event in which the Ford Escort Twin-Cam made its very first appearance in an international rally, and which took all the scribes' attention.

Although Abingdon then had to concentrate on the 1800s which it was preparing for the East African Safari, the

By 1968 the 'works' Mini was at the peak of its development – this is Paddy Hopkirk/Ron Crellin at the start of a special stage in the 1968 Monte Carlo Rally.

next two events in the Mini's calendar were the Circuit of Ireland and the Tulip Rally. In summary – and this has to be said – the Minis could so easily have won both events, if it had not been for the arrival of the Escort Twin-Cams, which won both events.

On the Circuit, Paddy Hopkirk's JMO 969D (not a 'lucky' car, as the records confirm) had been built as a lightweight Group 6 'racer' – lightweight panels, Weber carburettors and all – and was fighting head-to-head with Roger Clark's Escort for days, until the transmission differential failed. Julien Vernaeve and Timo Makinen were similarly competitive in the Tulip – until Timo went off the road on the Col de Brabant (in France). Ford's 150bhp Escorts took first (Clark – that man again) and second overall, but Vernaeve was always close behind them, and took third overall.

Now it was time for a really long-haul trip – for Paddy Hopkirk to compete in the six-day Shell 4000 Rally of Canada, which started from Calgary, and finished in Halifax, Nova Scotia. In spite of the colossal, 4000 mile (6440km), length of the event, there were only 155 miles (249.5km) of high speed special stages. As happened so often at Abingdon, Paddy's car – GRX 5D – was not all that it seemed, for the Group 1 MkI car which had started life on the 1966 Monte Carlo Rally had later been seen as a

The scene, a peaceful little French village, as Paddy Hopkirk (driving ORX 777F) scurries through on a road section of the 1968 Monte Carlo Rally.

full Group 2 car, then as 970cc race car in the 1967 Marathon de la Route, and was now clothed in a brand-new MkII bodyshell, with a 1293cc engine!

The author actually attended this event, and saw that although the car was competitive at first, it soon began to suffer from chronic overheating. Before long, and to keep it motoring until and unless the organisers threw it out, the car then ran with an extra water radiator strapped to the nose, in full view. Then it disappeared for a time, then re-appeared – and finally the car was disqualified. Although Paddy realised that this was inevitable, he pointed out that otherwise he would have had to retire at an early stage, and that he wanted to give the spectators and his supporters a show …

Then came the Acropolis, which the Mini had won in such fine style in 1967, this time there being two cars for the Flying Finns – Rauno Aaltonen and Timo Makinen – to drive, Rauno's being brand-new

Clean, smart, and clearly not in a hurry – this was Timo Makinen and Paul Easter on the run in towards Monte Carlo in the 1968 rally.

Timo Makinen and Paul Easter contested the 1968 Tulip in LBL 66D, a car which had started life in 1967 as a MkI machine, but had been turned into a fully-tuned Group 2 MkII by this time.

for the occasion. Unhappily, what had recently become BMC's Bogey Car – the Escort Twin-Cam – triumphed again, which left the Mini Cooper S-types struggling to keep up with the Escorts, and with the 'works' Porsche 911s. Although Rauno kept on, gamely, he had to settle for fifth overall, while Timo Makinen soon dropped out with engine overheating.

Could there be a change of fortune in the Scottish? Lars Ytterbring competed in the ex-Hopkirk Group 6 car from the Circuit of Ireland, and came very close to winning the hot, dusty and fast special-stage event outright, but eventually had to settle for second place behind … Roger Clark's Escort Twin-Cam.

Next, the team came very close to winning the Finnish 1000 Lakes Rally, where Timo Makinen made his last-ever appearance in a Mini Cooper S. Interesting, this – one eminent Mini historian assures us that Timo did not drive for BMC after the Acropolis, while another historian ignores the rally completely. Both are wrong – for Timo and Lars Ytterbring started, in ORX 77F and ORX 777F respectively, though both retired, Timo's car with electrical failure followed by a transmission breakage, and Ytterbring's car with broken suspension after jumping too high on one of Finland's notorious high-speed 'yumps.'

With Abingdon now committed to preparing five BMC 1800s for the London-Sydney Marathon, there was neither space, time nor money to send Minis off to many events in the autumn – and in fact, for the first time in many years, there would be no factory presence at the RAC Rally. After the 1000 Lakes expedition in August, only one other 'works' Mini started a rally – that being Paddy Hopkirk in the Portuguese TAP Rally in October. Here was another of those so-near/so-far outings which had inflicted the Mini in 1968, for Paddy (driving LBL 606D – originally a 1967 Monte Carlo Rally car, but strangely invisible since then) came very close to winning the event, though in the end he had to settle for second place overall.

This was the moment when Peter Browning had to let his team know that, on instructions from higher authority, the only driver who would be retained on a contract for 1969 was Paddy Hopkirk – for Rauno Aaltonen, Tony Fall and Timo Makinen had all to be 'released' … Peter was most unhappy about this, as naturally were the drivers themselves.

1969

For 1969, policies imposed from above by British Leyland meant that the Mini Cooper S disappeared almost completely from international rallies. Although the list of events entered was as high as ever, these were almost entirely rallycross, and circuit racing events. Compared with 1968, and in a complete reversal of strategy, during 1969 'works' Mini Cooper Ss contested just one major rally – the Circuit of Ireland – and the Tour de France, which was an exciting, hybrid, race/rally marathon.

Classic rallies such as Monte Carlo, the Acropolis and the French Alpine – all of which had more recently been won by 'works' Minis – were ignored. In the meantime, the team got on with the preparation and development of MG MGC GT race cars and started work on the Triumph 2.5 PI rally programme.

Early in the year, though, there seemed to be time, and some money, for one very special Mini to be built up for Paddy Hopkirk to use on the Circuit of Ireland. Because Paddy had lost out to Roger Clark's Ford Escort Twin-Cam in 1968, and because, after all, it was his 'home' event, Paddy looked on the Circuit as 'unfinished business,' and lobbied for the very best tarmac-rallying Mini which Abingdon could devise.

Fortunately for all concerned, the Circuit once again included a category for Group 6 (effectively 'Prototype') saloons where almost any modification (except a change of bodyshell, or of engine/transmission position) was authorised. Abingdon therefore set about building what was effectively a brand-new 1275S which incorporated everything they knew. Agreed, the registration number chosen – GRX 311D – was old (this identity had started its life on the 1966 Acropolis Rally, and had been used extensively in 1966 and 1967, though it had not figured at all in 1968), but as I have repeatedly pointed out in this series of books, such things mattered not at all to 'works' teams at the time.

The 'new' GRX 311D was a tarmac-special in all respects, being as light, as low, and as stripped out as possible. Not only was the basic bodyshell de-seamed, but every possible unstressed body panel was made out of aluminium instead of steel (such pressings had been used in the past, notably on the 1967 French Alpine), Perspex windows replaced glass (except for the screen), a magnesium alloy sump guard, by Minilite, was adopted, and a choice of 10in or 12in-diameter Minilite road wheels were made ready, with a variety of Dunlop tyres, some of them out-and-out racers.

After all the detailed preparation work which had been carried out, the story of this rally was one of frustration for Paddy and the mechanics. Not only did GRX 311D suffer from persistent bouts of engine misfiring (this was eventually cured, after whole-sale rebuilding of manifolds and carburetion at service points), but problems with the handling when the car was running on 12in wheels. At the end of the event, which had been dominated by Roger Clark in an extremely-special 1.8-litre Ford Escort Twin-Cam, Paddy brought the car home in second place overall, with Adrian Boyd third overall in a privately-prepared Mini Cooper S which included many 'Abingdon' special pieces.

As far as Mini-rallying was concerned, Abingdon then went into hibernation from April to September, when a simply massive effort went into preparing three brand-new 1275S cars for the nine day Tour de France. Although BMC knew all about this event – Paddy Hopkirk's exploits in the 1963 Tour (in 33 EJB) were still talked about, especially in France – they had not been back to the event since 1964, for the Tour had been in suspended animation since that year, for Shell had withdrawn their generous financial support. That five year lay-off, however, did not matter so much for BMC, since their latest 'endurance' race cars had performed so well in the 84-Hour Marathon de la Route in 1967. Peter Browning's team, accordingly, thought they knew what was needed.

Using three of the modern 1.3-litre race cars – OBL 45F, URX 550G and URX 560G – and with a team that included Paddy Hopkirk, John Handley and Brian Culcheth as first drivers, hopes were high. Because the various categories existed – and financial rewards for class success were still high – the team hedged every possible bet by asking Brian Culcheth to drive URX 550G in Group 1 (near standard) condition, John Handley's Group 5 car had a single Weber 45 DCOE carburettor instead of twin SUs, while Paddy's Group 5 car had fuel-injection like that of the latest race cars. Culcheth's Group 1 car ran on steel wheels, the others using fat wheel-arch extensions and knock-off type Minilite wheels. In addition, and to provide backing, Julien Vernaeve entered his own Group 1 car.

As revived under the control of one-time successful rally and race car driver Bernard Consten, the event started from Nice on 18th September, and eventually finished up in Biarritz, on the Biscay coast, close to the border with Spain. Because this was an event where there were entire fleets of Porsches, Ferraris, Alfa Romeos and Alpine-Renaults among the 106 starters, the 'works' Minis could not hope to be fighting for the outright lead, and could do no more than try to win their various classes.

As in 1964, this was a monstrously long and tough event, with six long legs, covering nine days, 5000km (approx 3100 miles), ten circuit races (not sprints, but out and out races), and eleven speed hill climbs. Also as in 1964 (the last time the Mini Coopers had attacked the Tour de France), the races were held, inter alia, at famous circuits such as Spa, the Nürburgring and Le Mans, while many of the hill climbs were well-known from major rallies, and included Mont Ventoux and the Ballon d'Alcase.

Although this was not altogether a happy event for the Group 5 Minis in the end, Paddy Hopkirk eventually finished a very creditable 14th overall, with no smaller-engined car ahead of him, and won his capacity class. After several hill climbs, along with races at Rouen, Rheims and Clermont-Ferrand, the Group 5 cars lay fourth and fifth in the Special Touring Car Category (Handley was just leading Hopkirk, though theoretically his carburetted car was less powerful …), because Paddy's car had been suffering from oil surge, and had needed a pit-stop in the Clermont race to have the sump topped up.

Paddy's car then suffered all manner of problems – first with a heater hose coming loose (which caused water loss), then when a front suspension arm came adrift on a road section, and eventually a broken valve spring, which was changed at the side of the road without lifting the cylinder head. Later he needed a plug change during the Nogaro circuit race, then punctured, and was not best pleased.

John Handley was even less lucky, for on the last-but-one hillclimb (the Col d'Aspin, in the Pyrenees) he mis-heard a pace note, crashed into a stone wall, and damaged the car severely. Since the car had been suffering from clutch slip for many hours, this was absolutely the last straw.

The Group 1 cars had a less eventful Tour, for both finished, first and second in their capacity class, with Vernaeve's suspiciously quick 'standard' Group 1 car ahead of Culcheth's machine. Two class wins and three of the four cars getting to the finish? It could have been worse. Team boss Peter Browning later wrote that: 'In all, the Tour was one of our more successful ventures, bringing back memories of the classic Hopkirk performance with the Mini in the 1963 event …'

Unhappily, for the Mini Cooper there would be no resurgence of success in 1970. Not only had Lord Stokes's British Leyland men continued their clamp down on rallying, but most of Abingdon's efforts, planning, and available funds went into building up a formidable team of Triumph 2.5PIs, and Austin Maxis, to compete in the London–Mexico World Cup Rally, which was sponsored so generously by the *Daily Mirror* newspaper.

Here was an event which would start from London, and journey via Sofia (in Bulgaria) to Lisbon. Having been shipped over the Atlantic by sea, the cars would then tackle an enormous month-long circuit of South and Central America, from Rio de Janeiro to Mexico City by way of Buenos Aires, Santiago and Lima. Special stages (called Primes) abounded, some of them well over 12 hours long, while the general challenge of distance was to be spiced up with endurance, awful road conditions and climatic extremes.

If the publicity staffs had not agreed to showcase a single Mini, as something of a trail blazer, there would have been nothing at all to link that famous event with Abingdon's most famous car. Almost as an afterthought, however, it was decided to prepare a single Mini for the event, one which would nominally be supported by the *BBC Grandstand* programme. Because the event ran to a distinctly relaxed set of regulations (the organisers, led by John Sprinzel, took the view that the sheer magnitude of the Marathon – the official length of the event was put at 16,244 miles (25,990.5km) – would limit the changes which team managers wanted to make), Abingdon could build the very best possible Mini for the job in hand.

No-one at Abingdon was under any illusions about this project, as it was never likely that a highly-tuned Mini could complete the enormous mileage. Accordingly, the team set out to produce the fastest and most promising car that they could, knowing that the remains might, just might, have to be returned to Abingdon in a trailer well before the finish. According to team boss Peter Browning, driver John Handley was ordered to: '... lead at Lisbon or bust ...' – and be prepared to come home early.

In the end, the choice of car fell on a much-modified square-nosed 1275GT – the model had been launched in the autumn of 1969, and would eventually take the place (in the price lists, if not in the hearts of enthusiasts) of the Mini Cooper S in the showrooms – into which every ounce of Abingdon expertise was crammed.

Even before the event began, the troubles started, for although John Handley carried out much testing, he and co-driver Paul Easter found their plans for a detailed reconnaissance of the European section frustrated by awful weather, which culminated in them being stranded in the Jugoslavian resort of Dubrovnik for three days on one occasion.

The rally car (XJB 308H) was brand-new, and took many painstaking weeks to be made ready. Based on the definitive specification of the existing 1275S, the 1293cc engine ran on twin SU carburettors, in full Downton-type

Paul Easter and children with the sole Clubman 1275GT, which was ready to start the World Cup Rally of 1970. This was an ill-fated car that soon retired with engine failure.

tune, and was claimed to produce 115bhp at the flywheel. Not only was an engine oil cooler tucked in behind the front grille, but there was a secondary water radiator too. The final drive ratio was 3.9:1, the usual 'comps' straight-cut gearbox cluster was chosen, and 12in diameter wheels with 6.0in rims were fitted. The bodyshell included a roll cage, and closing panels (doors, bonnet or boot lid) in aluminium and glass-fibre, with a huge extra bag fuel tank, by Autovita, to bring total capacity up to 22 gallons.

Everything, unhappily, seemed to go wrong with this car though. There was much trouble in pre-event testing and shakedown, it had to take second place in Abingdon's workshop priorities (behind the finalisation of the A-team of Triumphs), and on the event itself there were difficult-to-trace fuel starvation problems in the Balkans. In the end, too, the engine began to consume vast quantities of oil and it blew in a big way on a Prime in Italy (only four days after the event had started) – and, as gloomily forecast in advance – it never even had the chance to get as far as the start of the South American sections.

Although the World Cup entry itself was a write-off, the car was not entirely wasted. No sooner had the team got back from Mexico City (where, incidentally, Brian Culcheth's Triumph 2.5PI had finished second overall to Hannu Mikkola's victorious Ford Escort), than the Mini Cooper S (XJB 308H) was refurbished, a new engine was fitted, and the entire car was converted to something more akin to the usual Mini Cooper S 'sprint' specification, for Paddy Hopkirk to drive in the Scottish Rally.

Fortunately for all concerned, there was a Group 6 ('prototype') category on this event (this explains why Ford could enter Roger Clark in an Escort RS1600 before it was even homologated), so all the special features of the World Cup car could be retained. The huge bag fuel tank, though, had been removed. Paddy's previous difficult experiences with 12in wheels were repeated on this event, so in mid-rally, and at Paddy's request, the 1275GT soon reverted to conventional 10in Minilites instead.

This was to be Paddy's last drive for the BMC/British Leyland 'works' team, and it was almost, if not quite, a complete success. Always among the pace-setters, but never quite capable of setting fastest stage times, Paddy and the 1275GT eventually finished second overall, to Brian Culcheth's winning Triumph 2.5PI (which was the ex-'World Cup' test and development car).

[If Kallstrom's 'works' Lancia Fulvia 1.6HF had not run out of time on road schedules after taking a great deal of time in one service/rebuild, it would have been the winner, and Paddy would have been moved down one place, to third, but that was an 'if only' which British Leyland was happy to forget.]

As already noted, the programme then ended on a really downbeat note, for team boss Peter Browning's resignation, and the announcement of the department's imminent closure, shattered everyone's hopes for the future. Even so, although the closure of the Abingdon department had already been announced, two 'works' cars – one of them being a brand-new MkIII Mini Cooper S (YMO 881H), the other being RJB 327F (rebuilt, but an ex-Spa 24-Hours race car) – were shipped out, to compete down under, in Australia. Brian Culcheth and Andrew Cowan were to compete in the Southern Cross and the Rally of the Hills in October and November.

Unhappily, there was no fairy tale finish. Not only did Culcheth roll his car in a pre-Southern Cross 'shakedown' autocross, but both cars retired on the Southern Cross. Although Culcheth's car led at first, it then suffered from engine overheating (due to water loss) and, eventually, a blown head gasket, while Cowan's car broke a drive shaft after crashing into a bank. Rebuilt cars then tackled the Rally of the Hills, where Brian Culcheth took fourth place after taking the wrong route on one stage and, with it, the lead.

Both those cars were sold off, Down Under, and that was that.

Past its best? Which rivals took over?

By 1969, certainly by 1970, the rallying Mini Cooper S had really reached its peak, while other rival cars were still improving. Until and unless the eight-port cylinder head could be homologated, and fuel-injection made reliable, there was no more to come from the 1275cc (really 1293cc, in Group 2-prepared form), the gearbox (firmly encased in the sump, and therefore incapable of physical expansion) was already at its development limit, and very little encouraging progress had been made in trying to make the cars handle better on 12in road wheels. Even if British Leyland had encouraged further work on the car, it is doubtful if much more could have been wrung out of the design.

In the meantime, Stuart Turner's forecast of 1964 ('Take to the Hills – the Lotus-Cortina is coming …') had matured, the Lotus-Cortina had given way to the Escort Twin-Cam, and the rallying balance of power had changed: once Ford turned the new 16-valve Cosworth BDA into a reliable engine, it was certainly game over for Abingdon.

By this time, too, three other very different rival cars had started to dominate the results sheets – the Alpine-Renault A110, Lancia Fulvia HF and Porsche 911 – and the fully-developed Mini Cooper S really had no answer to any of them. The Alpine-Renault was lighter, more powerful, and with better traction on all surfaces, the Lancia was one size larger, but had a high-tech 1.6-litre engine and a great deal of Italian finance behind it, while the Porsche 911 (which was already up to 2.2 litres, and up to 180bhp in 1970) seemed to have quite limitless potential.

Many years on, the Rover Group celebrated Paddy Hopkirk's 1964 Monte win, by entering him in the 1994 Monte Carlo in a new Mini Cooper. Note the registration number – L33 EJB – which compared with the 33 EJB of the legendary 1964 model.

No British Leyland successor to the Mini Cooper

As already noted in the early section (The Car and The Team), before he resigned from his position of Competition Manager in the summer of 1970, Peter Browning was already finding it difficult to convince any of British Leyland's senior management of the worth of international rallying – or of the fact that 'homologation specials' (of which two cars – the Ford Escort RS1600 and the Lancia Fulvia 1.6HF – were perfect examples) would eventually overwhelm brave attempts to use modified versions of production cars.

If Peter had been allowed to develop a master plan, and a modest form of 'homologation special' had been approved, he would have settled on the 16-valve Triumph Toledo which was being considered (in the end, this became the much heavier, less-sporting, four-door Dolomite Sprint), along with a rather specialised version of the 3.5-litre V8-engined Rover 3500S, complete with a robust manual transmission. Neither project, however, ever got beyond the 'why don't we …?' stage.

The search for a successor was abandoned after Abingdon closed its doors. Although Basil Wales bravely made much out of very little at Special Tuning, he was

Keeping alive the tradition! Before they tackled the 1994 Monte in a newly-built Mini Cooper, Paddy Hopkirk (centre) and Ron Crellin (right), pose with PR consultant John Brigden. Behind them is a line-up of historic rally cars, including 33 EJB (1964 Monte winner), AJB 44B (1965 winner), and LBL 6D (1967 winner)!

obliged to use slightly-developed/ slightly-improved versions of existing cars, like the unpromising Morris Marina and Austin Allegro-types, and there was really no chance of any such car ever becoming a front-line rally car.

From the summer of 1970, the Glory Days of Abingdon were over, and it was not until the Competitions Department was re-formed in 1975 that Triumph Dolomite Sprint race and rally cars, and Triumph TR7/TR7 V8 rally cars became competitive, if not regular winning, cars.

Although AJB 44B was retired as soon as it had won the 1965 Monte Carlo Rally, many years later Austin Rover dug it out, and refurbished it, for Paddy Hopkirk and Brian Culcheth to use in the RAC's 1982 Golden Fifty Rally. Need one say that it won that event, too?

Opposite: In later years Minis and their drivers lived on, to dominate 'classic' rallying too. At the end of an early Pirelli Classic Marathon of the 1990s, which ended in Cortina in Italy, Paddy Hopkirk and Alec Poole drove 6 EMO (never a works car, but the identity was close …) to victory, ahead of Stirling Moss (MGB, on their right), and Ron Gammons/Paul Easter (MGB).

World/major European rally wins

All with 1275cc engines unless noted:
970 = 970cc Mini Cooper S; 997 = 997cc Mini Cooper; 1071 = 1071cc Mini Cooper S

Event	Car	Drivers
1962		
Tulip	737 ABL (997)	Pat Moss/Ann Wisdom
Baden-Baden (German)	737 ABL (997)	Pat Moss/Pauline Mayman
1963		
French Alpine	277EBL (1071)	Rauno Aaltonen/Tony Ambrose
1964		
Monte Carlo	33 EJB (1071)	Paddy Hopkirk/Henry Liddon
Tulip	AJB 66B	Timo Makinen/Tony Ambrose
1965		
Monte Carlo	AJB 44B	Timo Makinen/Paul Easter
Geneva	EBL 55C	Rauno Aaltonen/Tony Ambrose
Czech	EBL 55C	Rauno Aaltonen/Tony Ambrose
Polish	CRX 89B	Rauno Aaltonen/Tony Ambrose
1000 Lakes	AJB 33B	Timo Makinen/P Keskitalo
Munich-Vienna-Budapest	CRX 89B	Rauno Aaltonen/Tony Ambrose
RAC	DJB 93B	Rauno Aaltonen/Tony Ambrose
1966		
Monte Carlo	GRX 555D	Timo Makinen/Paul Easter **
Tulip	GRX 310D	Rauno Aaltonen/Henry Liddon
Austrian Alpine	DJB 93B	Paddy Hopkirk/Ron Crellin
Czech	JBL 494D	Rauno Aaltonen/Henry Liddon

Event	Car	Drivers
Polish	GRX 309D (970)	Tony Fall/Attis Krauklis
1000 Lakes	JBL 493D	Timo Makinen/P Keskitalo
Munich-Vienna-Budapest	HJB 656D	Timo Makinen/Paul Easter
1967		
Monte Carlo	LBL 6D	Rauno Aaltonen/Henry Liddon
Acropolis	LRX 830E	Paddy Hopkirk/Ron Crellin
Geneva	LRX 827E	Tony Fall/Mike Wood
1000 Lakes	GRX 195D	Timo Makinen/P Keskitalo
French Alpine	LRX 827E	Paddy Hopkirk/Ron Crellin

** Disqualified on a technicality at post-event scrutineering

Victories by 'works' Minis in British international rallies

Event	Car	Drivers
1965		
Circuit of Ireland	CRX 89B	Paddy Hopkirk/Terry Harryman
1966		
Circuit of Ireland	DJB 92B	Tony Fall/Henry Liddon
Scottish	DJB 93B	Tony Fall/Mike Wood
1967		
Circuit of Ireland	GRX 5D	Paddy Hopkirk/Terry Harryman

Visit Veloce on the web – www.veloce.co.uk
Details of all books in print • Special offers • New book news • Gift vouchers • Forum

119

Works rally cars (and when first used)

Mini Cooper and Mini Cooper S

These are the identities of the factory-prepared Mini Cooper and Mini Cooper S rally cars built and registered by BMC (British Motor Corporation) between 1962 and 1970, for use in major European events and British international events. In each case I have listed the first year in which they appeared.

Note that as structures wore out, or were crashed, some of these identities were 'cloned', and reappeared on newly-built cars, keeping their original registration plates, and chassis plates too. The confusion was that in later life, long discarded and 'worn-out' shells have been rescued, rebuilt, and re-created as so-called ex-works cars. In some cases, there is/was more than one claimant to a particular registration number/identity.

Unless noted, all cars listed were Mini Cooper S with 1275cc engines.

Where applicable, I have added important successes.

1962
737 ABL (997cc) (1st 1962 Tulip, 1st 1962 Baden-Baden)
407 ARX (997cc)
977 ARX (997cc)
477 BBL (997cc)

1963
17 CRX (997cc)
18 CRX (997cc)
8 EMO (1071cc)
277 EBL (1071cc) (1st 1963 French Alpine)
33 EJB (1071cc) (1st 1964 Monte Carlo)

1964
569 FMO (1071cc)
570 FMO (1071cc)
AJB 33B (1st 1965 1000 Lakes)
AJB 44B (1st 1965 Monte Carlo)
AJB 55B
AJB 66B (1st 1964 Tulip)
BJB 77B
CRX 89B (1st 1965 Circuit of Ireland, 1st 1965 Polish, 1st 1965 Three Cities)
CRX 90B
AGU 780B

1965
CRX 88B
CRX 91B
DJB 92B (1st 1966 Circuit of Ireland)
DJB 93B (1st 1965 RAC, 1st 1966 Austrian Alpine, 1st 1966 Scottish)
EJB 55C (1st 1965 Czech)
EBL 55C (1st 1965 Geneva)
EBL 56C

1966
GRX 5D (1st 1967 Circuit)
GRX 55D
GRX 195D (1st 1967 1000 Lakes)
GRX 309D (1st 1966 Polish – running as a 970S)
GRX 310D (1st 1966 Tulip)
GRX 311D

GRX 555D (1st 1966 Monte, but disqualified on a
    scrutineering technicality)
HJB 656D (1st 1966 Three Cities)
JBL 172D
JBL 493D (1st 1966 1000 Lakes)
JBL 494D (1st 1966 Czech)
JBL 495D
JMO 969D

1967
LBL 6D (1st 1967 Monte)
LBL 66D
LBL 606D
LBL 666D
LBL 590E
LRX 827E (1st 1967 Geneva, 1st 1967 French Alpine)
LRX 828E
LRX 829E
LRX 830E (1st 1967 Acropolis)

1968
ORX 7F

ORX 77F
ORX 707F
ORX 777F
OBL 46F
RBL 450F

1969
OBL 45F
RJB 327F
URX 550G
URX 560G

1970
SOH 878H (Mini Clubman 1275GT)
XJB 308H (Mini Clubman 1275GT)
YMO 881H
YMO 885J (Mini Clubman 1275GT) – but never used
YMO 886J (Mini Clubman 1275GT) – but never used

If we measure the total number of different cars based on registration numbers, there were 63, but rebuilds and reshells must have increased that total considerably.

Visit Veloce on the web – www.veloce.co.uk
Details of all books in print • Special offers • New book news • Gift vouchers • Forum

121

Index

Note: There are so many mentions of all models of the Mini on individual pages that they have not been indexed.

Visit Veloce on the web – www.veloce.co.uk
Details of all books in print • Special offers • New book news • Gift vouchers • Forum

124

RALLY GIANTS™

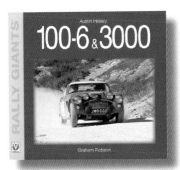

ISBN: 978-1-845841-28-7

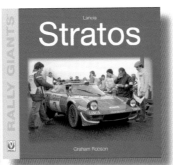

ISBN: 978-1-845840-41-9

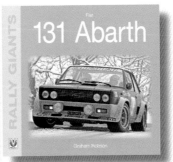

ISBN: 978-1-845841-82-9

ISBN: 978-1-845841-29-4

ISBN: 978-1-845840-42-6

ISBN: 978-1-845841-41-6

ISBN: 978-1-845840-40-2

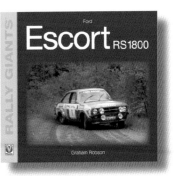

ISBN: 978-1-845841-40-9

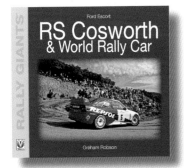

ISBN: 978-1-845841-81-2

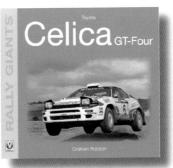

ISBN: 978-1-84584-184-3

**More great
titles
available
soon ...**

Anatomy of the Works Minis
Paperback • 25x20.7cm • £16.99*
• 96 pages • 77 photos
• ISBN: 978-1-903706-03-9

How the giant-killing Minis of rallying, rallycross & racing fame were converted from standard Mini Coopers in the BMC Competitions Department. The author, who spent 22 years in 'Comps,' reveals the secrets of specification, build technique and development of the famous Works Minis.

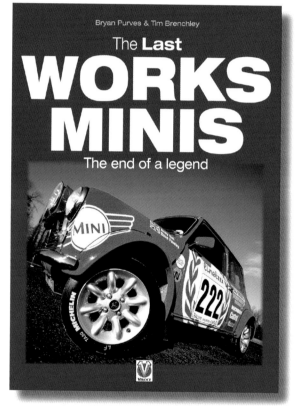

The Last Works Minis
Hardback • 23.8x17cm • £29.99*
• 304 pages • 500+ mainly colour photos
• ISBN: 978-1-845840-87-7

The story of the Works Mini's 'second coming' to compete in modern rallying and racing. Includes previously unpublished photos of the car's development, copies of Rover's internal documents, and pages from the road books of top rallies.

"The definitive guide to the Rover works Minis of 1993 to 1997 as entered by British Motor Heritage in rallies and races. Over 300 pages of history, detail and never seen before pics. Wallow in the Classic Mini's final blast as a works motorsport entry and let the good, and not so good, times roll." Review from *MiniWorld*, January 2008

How to Power Tune Minis on a Small Budget
Paperback • 25x20.7cm • £17.99*
• 112 pages • 50+ mainly colour pictures
• ISBN: 978-1-904788-84-3

Learn the secrets of how to use inexpensive, 'bolt-on' parts – readily available from Austin-Rover dealers, automotive suppliers & scrapyards (junkyards) – to increase the performance of all road-going Minis.

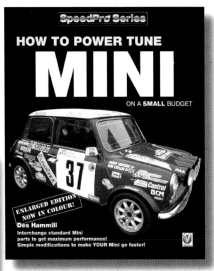

RAC Rally Action!
Hardback • 25x25cm • £35.99*
• 208 pages • 330 colour & b&w photos
• ISBN: 978-1-903706-97-8

This book covers the pre-WRC golden years, the Rally of the Forests period. With access to crew notes & manufacturers' archives, & containing many previously unpublished pictures, the history and excitement of the RAC International Rally of Great Britain has been captured forever by Tony Gardiner's book.

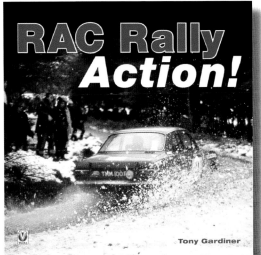

BMC Competitions Department Secrets
Hardback • 25x20.7cm • £24.99*
• 192 pages • 205 photos and illustrations
• ISBN: 978-1-904788-68-3

Three Competitions Department Managers reveal the inner workings & long-held secrets of one of the most prominent motorsport teams Britain has ever seen. Internal memos, highs & lows, and politics. Be prepared: much of this is sensational!

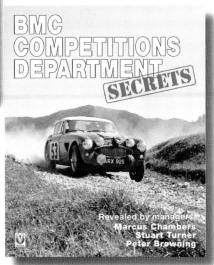

For more information on these and other great Veloce titles:
visit www.veloce.co.uk • email info@veloce.co.uk • or call +44 (0)1305 260068

* p+p extra, price subject to change

How to Build a Successful Low-Cost Rally Car
Paperback • 25x20.7cm • £16.99*
• 96 pages • 150 colour pictures
• ISBN: 978-1-845842-08-6

Simple, cost-effective, basic and reliable tips to ensure any rally car stands a chance of reaching the finishing line. If you are planning a road-based rally, don't even think of leaving home before reading this book and implementing the tried and tested mods it describes so well.

Mini
Paperback • 19.5x13.9cm • £9.99*
• 64 pages • 100 colour photos
• ISBN: 978-1-845842-04-8

Having this book in your pocket is just like having a real marque expert by your side. Benefit from the author's years of Mini ownership, learn how to spot a bad car quickly and how to assess a promising one like a true professional. Get the right car at the right price!

Works rally Mechanic
Paperback • 25x20.7cm • £16.99*
• 160 pages • 159 colour & b&w photos
• ISBN: 978-1-904788-18-8

For 22 years Brian prepared cars for international rallies, providing service support for 'Big' Healeys, Minis & TR7s. Adventure, hilarious events, hardship, winning, losing, & real danger …

"The stories that this 22-year veteran of the Abingdon-based British Motor Corporation/British Leyland Competitions Department shares chronicle the evolution of the 'works,' and the corporate policies that shaped its existence … fans of BMC/British Leyland cars will also enjoy a treasure of rarely seen photographs, many of which came from the personal collections of the author and his co-workers; 'Works Rally Mechanic' is a must for any Anglophile's bookshelf." Review from *Hemmings Sports & Exotic Car*, September 2007